The Universal Priesthood of Believers

Watchman Nee

CHRISTIAN FELLOWSHIP PUBLISHERS, INC.
NEW YORK

ISBN: 978-1-68062-081-8

Available from the Publishers at:

11515 Allecingie Parkway
Richmond, Virginia 23235
www.c-f-p.com

Printed in the United States of America

The
Universal Priesthood
of
Believers

PREFACE

This series of spoken ministry on the overall theme of the priesthood of all believers in Christ was delivered by Watchman Nee in Shanghai, China. They were spoken just prior to his convening on Mt. Kuling of what became the first of two Training Conferences for brother Nee's fellow workers, this one held during the late spring and summer of 1948. These spoken messages were meant to serve as a preparation for the said Training Conference which began almost immediately thereafter on Mt. Kuling, located a short distance inland from the port city of Foochow.

It is a pity that this Biblical truth of the universal priesthood of Christian believers is not being practiced among most of God's people today. And hence, these messages are very important, and should be carefully and prayerfully read.

Originally delivered in Chinese in the early spring of 1948, hand notes were taken at that time, and they have now been translated and published in English for the first time so that all who read them may be spiritually profited. It should be further noted that in preparing this translation for today's publication, numerous additional Scripture verses have been inserted here and there throughout this entire book's text where it was deemed necessary and/or helpful to the reader.

Contents

Chapter One

The Sympathy of the Great High Priest

> For we have not a high priest not able to sympathise with our infirmities, but [the Lord Jesus was] tempted in all things in like manner, sin apart. Let us approach therefore with boldness to the throne of grace, that we may receive mercy, and find grace for seasonable help.
>
> Hebrews 4:15-16

While the Lord Jesus walked on earth, He experienced all kinds of trial and temptation. When He suffered, He felt pain. When He was misunderstood, He sensed hurt. He had experienced many pains, He had suffered many persecutions. When He encountered all kinds of trials, He suffered feelings similar to what we all have felt. Hence, He is able to sympathize with our weaknesses.

Our Lord sympathizes with human weaknesses, but He never sympathizes with sin: "sin apart," says Hebrews. Indeed, the Lord Jesus had been tempted in all things such as we are, sin apart. We are never told in Scripture that He sympathizes with our sins, therefore He forgives us. No, He sympathizes with our human weaknesses, including having sympathy with the suffering which results from our fleshly weakness. What is the weakness of our flesh? It is the weakness which stems from our flawed soul. Towards such weakness He is sympathetic. We experience pains in our flesh—which is to say that our soul suffers pain. And towards such pains, the Lord Jesus is sympathetic.

To say that the Lord sympathizes means that He feels what we suffer. Have you ever felt such feelings? Have you ever shown sympathy towards others? You may have often been helped by others when in pain, yet you may have expressed no sympathy towards them in *their* pain: you manifested no feeling of the pain they were experiencing. In fact, when you saw someone in need, you may have met his need in some tangible way, but you did not sense the hardness—the difficulty—of his life. Yes, you see a person in sickness, and you may actually give him food to eat, clothes to wear, and nurse him back to health, yet your senses did not identify themselves with his pain. Outwardly you seem to be quite gracious and helpful, but inwardly you have no sympathy—that is, you do not feel as he does.

Jesus is the Lord of grace. He is the Sympathetic One. In this regard the Bible provides two characteristics possessed by the Lord: one is, He is Savior of sinners; the other, He is the Friend of sinners (Matthew 11:19). As Savior, He redeems sinners. As Friend, He has social intercourse with sinners. In this latter respect Jesus feels all the unbearable pains of sinners. Thank and praise God, the Lord Jesus is not only the sinners' Savior, He is also the sinners' Friend. By this we discern here the riches of His glory.

Sometimes you encounter difficulties, and so you feel lonely. Certain facial expressions in others trouble you, certain sounds in their voices hurt you. All your surroundings seem gray and depressing to you. But you need to know that while you experience these floods of pain, hurt and suffering, the Lord is not only your Savior, He is also your Friend who has the same feeling and experiences the same troubling and hurtful environment as you do.

Showing sympathy was a special feature of the Lord Jesus while He was on earth. The Bible records many occasions of how the Lord manifested His sympathy towards the people. He sympathized with the sick and healed them (e.g., Mark 6:56, Luke 4:40). He sympathized with the hungry and fed them—feeding on two occasions the five thousand people and the four thousand people, respectively (Mark 6:34-44, 8:1-9). He heard the cry of the blind man, "Son of David, have mercy on me," and healed the man. He beheld the sorrow expressed for the dead man Lazarus and caused him to be resurrected (Mark 10:46-52, John 11:37-44). Oh, if our hearts are truly open, we shall see how the Lord's sympathy graciously comes to us! Before He comes to be the sinners' Savior, He has been the sinners' Friend. True, we who are His people have well understood that Jesus came to the world to die. And yet, we would naturally think that if one's commission is to die, then nothing should matter except that that one should fulfill his destined death. Not so with the Lord Jesus. For even though the destined cross-experience was ever before Him and that He was always heading physically and mentally towards that death, He nonetheless was constantly sympathetic towards all who were in need of His help and assistance. Oh, how merciful and how much the Friend is our Lord!

For you who would be sympathetic towards sinners, you would need to possess at least three characteristics. And first would be experience: before you can sympathize, you must first have experience. If you have never been sick, you cannot sympathize with the sick. If you have never had a toothache, you cannot relate to those with the pain of a toothache. If you have never had a headache, you cannot commiserate with anyone gripped by a pounding headache. If you yourself continually seek to avoid any form of pain or suffering, you are not able to be sympathetic with the sufferer. Hence, experience is absolutely necessary for you to be sympathetic.

A sister in the Lord once said: "Many things I could not overcome, in many things I was defeated; and later on I sought advice from many believers who seemed to be better in the Christian life than I; yet, they could not understand my difficulties—as though they were born perfect saints. Indeed, they never seemed to have experienced any pain of defeat."

This underscores why I say that people without experience cannot sympathize with others.

Why is it that Jesus did not come to the world as a grown-up but had to pass through a woman's womb and experience being fed and growing up gradually? Why did He need to pass through more than thirty years of the growing-up process? Why—in order to accomplish the work of salvation—was He not crucified after being merely three days on earth? Oh, the reason He needed to pass through all such things as we do was for the purpose that He might be able to sympathize with us.

He suffered pain, agonies, grief, misunderstandings and persecutions. He was beaten, despised, and deserted by men, and eventually was crucified by men. He suffered every kind of bitterness of life so that He might sympathize with human weakness. Jesus' living as a man for over thirty years, His wandering about for some three years in preaching and teaching—all was for the purpose of not only fulfilling His mission of salvation, but also for the sake of coming into possession of a sympathetic heart. Jesus must go through life in this way in order that He would be able to sympathize with our frailty and weakness.

If there is anyone who has a broken heart or a wounded soul, here is the Lord Jesus who can feel with you and show you grace and mercy. He knows your feeling, your loneliness, your grief and sorrow. He not only is able to save you; He also is the Friend who has a sympathetic heart for you. In short, He identifies with your humanity and feels what you feel.

In order for anyone to sympathize with you, however, experience alone is not enough. The second necessary characteristic to have is love. Suppose a person has been sick for many years. He may need to lie down at times during those many years for a period of two whole days at a stretch. But though he knows how painful is his situation, he is not able to be sympathetic with all the sick people in the world: he can only be sympathetic towards his loved ones. Yes, indeed, he has much sick experience, yet he does not have love. So he is unable to sympathize with all people. Jesus, though, is able to show sympathy to all. And why? It is because He not only has experience but also has love. We may recall that on one occasion, as the Lord was coming down from a mountain, a leper approached and pleaded with Him by saying, "If You will, You can cleanse me." Jesus immediately touched this "unclean" man with His hand and said to him, "I am willing. Be thou cleansed" (see Matthew 8:1-3). The Lord could sense and feel the pain of the leper. And hence, He touched the leprous man with His hand. Oh, our Lord has not only experience, His heart is full of love.

Nevertheless, having experience and love are still inadequate for anyone who would be a sympathizer with others who are hurting. The third essential characteristic for the Lord to have is that He himself must have nothing personally bothering Him that would prevent His being able, willing and interested to sympathize with others and reach out to them. Which is to say, that nothing had seized hold of Him first. Let us contrast that with ourselves. Many times our minds and hearts have become totally occupied with other things already. And thus, being much preoccupied, our hearts become closed up, unable—even unwilling and unconcerned—to express love or sympathize with others in their pain, grief or suffering. Instead, we would claim that we ourselves are burdened down and heavily laden; so our hearts are preoccupied and we are thus unable to sympathize with the burdens and needs of others. We would defensively say that our own burdens are themselves wellnigh unbearable; so how can anyone expect us to show love and sympathy towards others?

However, when the Lord was on earth, He constantly demonstrated the loving characteristic of being able to ignore and forget His own need. Indeed, what He was able to *not* do was much more marvelous than what He was able and willing to do or to think. For instance, when He was hungry, He did not turn stones into bread to satisfy His hunger (Matthew 4:1-4). Again, when His enemies came to arrest Him, he did not—as He himself said He *could* do—ask the Father to send twelve legions of angels to protect Him (Matthew 26:47-53). Jesus did not think of himself; nor was His heart taken captive to His own affairs, so as to be unable or unwilling to sympathize with the need, burden or pain of others. Too often we become captive to our burdens, sorrows, and pain to such an extent that we lose our feelings of love and sympathy when we see others' sufferings.

Not so with the Lord Jesus. Had He thought, while on the cross, of only His own suffering situation, and had thus been taken captive altogether by His personal agony and suffering, He would have had no place in His heart for expressing concern and sympathizing with others (Luke 23:39-43). During His latter years of life on earth, had His mind and heart dwelt solely upon the sufferings He was well aware He was going to suffer, He would have been taken captive daily by those sufferings (which, incidentally, were the greatest sufferings of all mankind), and hence He would have been unable to address the needs and sufferings of others, which thing He unhesitatingly did do continually. For the Lord Jesus spent all His days caring for others as though nothing else mattered. He healed the sick when He was with them, He preached the gospel when He met the poor. There seemed to have been nothing burdensome bothering Him, in that He showed sympathy no matter in what circumstance He found himself: He showed sympathy, concern and love to all. On each occasion when confronted with the need and suffering in others He expressed heartfelt sympathy. In fact, Jesus' heart was like a blank canvas upon which any image of the pain and suffering of others could be impressed. Praise and thank the Lord, His heart was—and still is—ever open to the need of others.

Jesus not only was sympathetic towards the people on earth in His day, even today He is sympathetic *towards us*. He is our

Great High Priest, who is now in heaven expressing unending sympathy with us in our suffering, pain, or grief; for what He had experienced of those same things while on earth was a thousand times more difficult than what we today experience. We can therefore trust Him wholly.

Whatever difficulty you may have, the Lord Jesus can relate to you. Our Great High Priest will give you grace to support you and give you peace; for did we not read earlier this tremendous promise from God's word: "Let us approach therefore with boldness to the throne of grace, that we may receive mercy, and find grace for seasonable needs." Oftentimes you may think people do not consider your situation as anything serious, and that there is no one to sympathize with you and extend help. At such times, you sense the heaviness of your burden and your heart is greatly pained. But there is One in heaven who sympathizes with you and is ready to sustain you.

Therefore, do not hesitate to come to the throne of grace and ask of the Lord, who indeed sympathizes with you. He wholeheartily cares for you and will lighten your burden. Friends of yours on earth may at times try, unsuccessfully in some instances, to lighten your burden, but your Friend in heaven is always ready, able and willing to lighten that burden. He does not only *lighten* your pained feeling, your agony or grief, He actually *bears* that burden of yours. He not only takes pity on you, He also takes care of you. In fact, He who is in heaven seems to have *you* solely in mind, and thus He is able to show you the utmost personal care. He is such a great and gracious High Priest. We praise and thank God for giving us such a blessed Friend and Savior.

Finally, I want to leave you with this thought: that because Jesus is such a gracious Friend who sympathizes with you, He will never place an unbearable burden on you. You need to remember that in whatever circumstance, position or situation you find yourself, He is always with you. Our Great High Priest senses your every feeling of grief, sadness or pain, and will always show mercy towards you. He senses deeply your every need and appreciates your every tear. Accordingly, let us trust the Lord and experience His gracious sympathy. Though He is not here on earth today, nevertheless, His heart always remains here with us.

Chapter Two

Priesthood

... and ye shall be to me a kingdom of priests, and a holy nation.

Exodus 19:6a

In the Bible we read that there is an office called the priesthood. This office is maintained by nothing else but a group of people who have been wholly separated from the world in order that they may serve God exclusively. Such a group of people do nothing but serve God. And the Bible calls such people priests.

History of Priesthood

Beginning in the time of Genesis God already had His priest—Melchizedek. He was God's very first priest. At the time of Abraham this Melchizedek separated himself especially to serve God. Commencing from the time of Genesis till after the establishment of the nation of Israel there were priests. Moreover, from the time of the Lord Jesus till the moment He left the world, there were also priests. Thus, the priesthood continued on for a very long period. The Bible also tells us that after the resurrection of the Lord Jesus, He also became a priest—in fact, *the* Priest—before God. In other words, ever since then the Risen and Ascended Lord Jesus has been before God the Father totally serving Him.

Furthermore, during the entire history of the church and right up to today, we see that this priestly office has continued on without ceasing.

Looking ahead to the moment when the millennium begins, we also learn from the Bible that those who shall have part in the first resurrection will likewise be priests—both to God and to Christ. Also, these same people shall be kings with Christ during this same thousand-year period (Revelation 20:6). In other words, during the millennial era, the children of God will continually be priests to God and Christ. Towards the world they will be kings, towards God and Christ Jesus they shall be priests whose priesthood shall not change.

On the other hand, at the time of the new heaven and new earth, the word priest shall no longer exist. Instead, from that time forward, all God's children will be called God's servants; and they shall do nothing but serve God. Hence, in the city of New Jerusalem, all God's servants will serve Him.

So we here have briefly contemplated a most wonderful circumstance, that Biblical priesthood began from Melchizedek —who had no chronology (he having no beginning nor end, see Hebrews 7:3)—and will last right up through the end of the millennial period; nevertheless, its essential meaning shall continue throughout eternity.

The Kingdom of Priests

From what we learn from the Bible, it would appear as though only Melchizedek was a priest. Yet, so far as God's purpose is concerned, priesthood is not meant only for one or two persons; His will is for all His people to be priests.

After the children of Israel came out of Egypt, they traveled to Mount Sinai, where God wanted Moses to tell the children of Israel: "And ye shall be to me a kingdom of priests, and a holy nation. These are the words which thou shalt speak to the children of Israel" (Exodus 19:6). God told the Israelites that they were a kingdom of priests. This word seemed not to have been easily understood. What did God mean by saying that His chosen people were to be a kingdom of priests? It simply meant that all the people in that nation were considered by Him to be priests. To explain the meaning further, among this nation of people there were to be no commoners; on the contrary, each

18

and every one comprising the whole nation was deemed by God to be a priest. I would say to you that this is His will.

When God chose the children of Israel to be His people, He had but one message to put before them, which was: that this nation was to be different from all the other nations of the world, that this nation was to be a kingdom of priests, signifying that all the people of this kingdom were to be priests. To put it another way, it meant that everyone had the same profession—that of serving God. Indeed, God desires for men to serve Him, He loves to have people on earth who will live solely for His will and purposes. In other words, God wants all His children to be priests who only serve Him.

So when the children of Israel arrived at Mount Sinai, God quickly notified them of this desire and purpose in choosing them as His people: "I will make you a kingdom of priests." I would declare to all of us here today that this is a wonderful announcement. We often call England a naval kingdom; the United States, a dollar kingdom; China, an ethical kingdom; and India, a philosophical kingdom. But here was a nation that was called a priestly kingdom. How wonderful that was! For in this kingdom no one was *not* to be a priest. In God's mind the men are priests, the women are priests, even the children are priests: everyone is a priest. All in this kingdom were to do nothing else but serve God. Apart from serving Him, people in this nation, including men, women and children, were to do nothing else. What a wonderful development this was.

After God had told the Israelites that they were to be a kingdom of priests, He then told Moses to come to the top of Mount Sinai and he would receive the Ten Commandments—written on two tables of stone—for the children of Israel to observe. Moses spent forty days at the summit. God himself was the one who inscribed these commandments on those two stone tablets. The first commandment called for the people not to worship other gods. The second commandment called for

19

them not to make any graven image, etc., etc.; and so it seemed that God had written them all, one by one.

Now when Moses ended up remaining on the mountain for seemingly a very long time, the people at the base of the mountain did not know what had happened to him. So, they ultimately said to Aaron—"Up, make us a god who will go before us." Unfortunately for the people, Aaron listened to them, gathered together from them lots of gold, and made a golden calf. Whereupon, the people worshiped the calf, with the people saying: "Israelites, this is the god who led us out of Egypt" (see Exodus 32:4b).

They began to worship that idol, sitting themselves down to eat and standing themselves up to play. There they greatly rejoiced over what had occurred because now they had a visible golden god to embrace as their own, since the God whom Moses caused them to know had in their eyes become distant and somewhat inconvenient, for it was not known what had become of Him, they finding it most difficult to search out and find Him. In fact, even Moses—the one who had led them forth out of Egypt for the purpose of worshiping God—could currently not be found (Exodus 32:1). So now they had a visible golden calf to worship. Sad to say, therefore, though God had called them to be priests solely for himself, they at this time had become priests serving a golden calf. Before even becoming a kingdom of priests to God, they had quickly begun to serve a golden calf idol. They today had replaced Jehovah God with a different god that had now become their object of worship (Exodus 32:4).

It would appear that the world's peoples have always nourished such an attitude towards their Creator God. They have always seemed bent on trying to create their own gods to worship. Instead of accepting the authority of their Creator and honoring His rightful position as the one true God, they would rather worship a god which they themselves create.

The Priestly Tribe

While Moses was yet atop Sinai, God instructed him to leave His presence and descend to the bottom of the mountain. But while descending, Moses carried in his hands the two tablets of law—the Ten Commandments—which God had himself inscribed. As he approached the Israelite camp, he beheld the people's awful condition and immediately became angry. He smashed the two tablets, then stood at the entrance of the camp, and announced: "He that is for Jehovah, let him come to me!" And all the ones of the tribe of Levi gathered to him. Then Moses commanded the Levites: "Put every man his sword upon his hip; and go and return from gate to gate through the camp, and slay every man his brother, and every man his friend, and every man his neighbor." They were to slay whoever they met, for those they encountered had worshiped the golden calf idol. No matter what the relationship might be, the Levites were to slay those people with their swords (Exodus 32:7-29).

Many may think that this was action far too extreme, for who would want to slay his own brother, his own close friend? Nevertheless, eleven among the twelve tribes did not respond to Moses' command, for they felt that such action was too costly to carry out. As a result, the Levites were alone in slaying from one side of the camp to the other. Altogether, they killed about three thousand people, all of whom were either their relatives, neighbors, or friends.

Please note that God immediately spoke to Moses after this golden calf affair and made it clear in so many words that the nation of Israel could not now be a kingdom of priests; for though this word was never specifically uttered by God, nonetheless, thereafter He gave the priesthood with all its service to the tribe of Levi alone (cf. Exodus 32:22-28). As we have seen, originally, this priesthood had been given to the entire nation of Israel, but now, it was to be given solely to Aaron's household and the rest of the tribe of Levi.

21

This thus signified that henceforth there would be two kinds of people in the nation of Israel: one was the people of God, the other, the priests of God. God's original purpose had been to make every one of His children a priest, because He did not want to separate the priesthood and its service from His people as a whole. God wanted all the people in the entire nation as priests. His people and His priests were to be one and the same. So long as you were one of God's people, you were automatically one of His priests. It was not to be the case that any of God's people would not be a priest.

But because many people love the world and care so much about human affections, they ultimately abandon their faithfulness to God and begin to worship idols; with the result that the children of God and the priests of God end up becoming two separate classes of people. Unless we love the Lord more than parents, wives, children, brothers, sisters, etc., we are not fit, said the Lord Jesus, to be His disciples (Luke 14:26). Many of God's people cannot meet or measure up to such a qualification, resulting in the children of God and the priests of God becoming two separate classes of believers.

Originally it was to be a whole nation of priests that would serve God, now it had become just a single tribe of priests who would do so. Formerly it was a nation of priests, now it would simply become a house of priests, in that the priesthood would now become a family affair. Let us please note that within the tribe of Levi, God's people and God's priests were one; for among the Levites, to be people of God meant that they automatically were the priests of God. Among the other eleven tribes, however, the Israelites were only God's people, they could not also be His priests. Needless to say, this had become a most serious matter, because when a person believes in the Lord he becomes one of God's people, and therefore, for him not to be His priest as well constitutes a most serious circumstance.

The Priesthood

From the time of the Exodus narrative concerning the golden calf affair till the time of the earthly presence of the Lord Jesus, the tribe of Levites was the only one among Israel's twelve tribes which had the priesthood; which thus meant that the people of these eleven tribes could not offer up sacrifices for themselves to God. They instead needed to ask the Levitical priests to offer up for them. They could not even confess their sins before God directly but had to ask the priests of Levi to confess for them. They could not separate themselves from the world. They were not able to touch the anointing oil (a symbol of God's Spirit) with their fingers. They had to ask the Levitical priests to anoint them that they might be separated from the world. They had to ask the one tribe of priests among themselves to do all spiritual things on their behalf.

Hence, during Old Testament times the children of Israel—those of the eleven tribes—had a distinctly special identity and status: for them God was afar off, He not being able to be reached by any of them directly. According to the record of the Old Testament their only recourse by which to reach out to God was solely via the Levitical priestly system. Indeed, I would call that system an intermediate one, in that the Israelites could not communicate with God directly but must go through their Levitical priests and God could only come to them through those same priests. Thus, between God and His chosen people there was now established an intermediate class.

According to God's original purpose there was never any such notion of a "go-between" class, since His original thought had been to come into their midst directly and likewise they to God directly. Now, though, with the emergence of the golden calf event, this was changed in favor of an intermediate priestly class—the tribe of Levi.

The Change in Priesthood

From the time of Moses till the time of the coming of the Lord Jesus—for almost fifteen hundred years—God's people could not approach Him directly. Only one family now served as priests. Because the people must pass through them to God, if anyone approached God directly, he would be struck dead immediately. Which meant that during that lengthy period of time priesthood constituted an extremely great and unique ministry. Eventually, however, came the New Covenant. People were redeemed and got saved. And in time we are given to read the words which announced: "Yourselves also, as living stones, are being built up a spiritual house, a holy priesthood, to offer spiritual sacrifices acceptable to God by Jesus Christ" (I Peter 2:5).

Here, Peter tells us that the foundation of the entire church is Christ, and that He as the Stone which the builders rejected has become the chief cornerstone (2:7). And, also noted the apostle, you are all living stones, being joined together and built up into a spiritual house. Here, therefore, we are told that all the redeemed are God's priests. All who serve in connection with the spiritual temple—the church of Christ—are priests.

Suddenly we notice that God, who had originally brought forth a purpose that shortly afterwards had been set aside for fifteen hundred years, has now taken up that purpose once again. What the children of Israel had forfeited is regained in the church. The children of Israel back then had forfeited the universal priesthood, but today it is regained by means of the New Covenant, as has been thoroughly presented in the New Testament. A word suddenly came forth from heaven to us which proclaimed that this universal priesthood has been regained by all the saved people of God.

The first chapter of Revelation (v. 6a) has made known the same news: "Made us a kingdom" (a more accurate translation of the Greek original). Not the word "people" here, but "kingdom." Originally, all throughout the kingdom of Israel were to be priests, but very soon they forfeited the concept and potential practice of the universal priesthood of God's chosen people. Today, however, the church is a nation of priests. What the children of Israel had lost in the presence of the golden calf idol, the church has wholly regained from the time of the earthly and ascended presence of the Lord Jesus. Today all the members of the church are priests. The original thought of a nation of priests as ordained by God has been fully recovered.

That which God had not been able to establish among the Israelites because of their disobedience is now established in the church. Today the church is a kingdom of priests because all in the church are priests. What does that mean? This is to say that the entire body of Christ, with its many members who have received the grace of God, has only one profession, and that is, serving God. I have repeatedly said the following to the young people: Before one believed in the Lord Jesus, being a physician or nurse or teacher was his or her only profession. The same with respect to a farmer or a businessman: farming or trading was that person's profession prior to believing in the Lord Jesus. Now, though, please understand that after a person has believed in the Lord Jesus, that one's profession undergoes a total change; for today all Christians have but one profession, which is, to serve God.

Upon our receiving Jesus as our Lord and Savior we become the priests of God. Whatsoever we may thereafter be busily involved in in terms of a livelihood, we nonetheless are serving God. To be a physician is now only for the purpose of maintaining a living; one's real profession is none other than to be a priest before God. The same will be true of the teacher, whose aim after receiving the Lord will not be to become a famous professor but to be a good priest of God. So shall it be with the merchant or farmer. All these are today merely side jobs, with our chief profession henceforth being to serve God.

May we lay down our ambitions with respect to our former professions. May we be like Paul whose special ambition was to please the Lord (Philippians 1:20-22). Apart from that there is no other ambition to be pursued by the Christian.

The Glory of the Priest

When not long after I myself had believed in the Lord Jesus, I began to feel that I needed to use a lot of strength to help keep a newly-saved believer serving God. In fact, I would beg him and persuade him to serve the Lord well. Let me say here, however, that God's thought is altogether different from ours. When the children of Israel sinned, God immediately took away priesthood from them. For from God's viewpoint, serving Him is the greatest privilege as well as the highest glory a believer can have. If people should fail, God will take away priesthood from them. In the case of the Israelites He did not persuade them or seek to please them. This is because being His priests is the servants' glory, not God's glory.

So please bear in mind that when the people of Israel offered strange fire, they were instantly stricken dead (Leviticus 10:1-2), or if they would ever enter the most holy place, they would immediately die; or if they should themselves offer up sacrifices, they would surely die (Numbers 17:13-18:7). In other words, apart from the priests, God would not permit anyone to approach Him directly. For from God's viewpoint, to be a priest was a glory which He himself granted to him. To be a priest back then was to be lifted up and elevated in status by God. If anyone should reach out to God according to his own idea, that one would end in death. For instance, when the ark of God accidentally fell while being transported and human hands tried to handle and steady it, immediately the man who did so was stricken to death (II Samuel 6:5-7).

Many people think that if they offer themselves to God, that act of service would uplift God. Not so. During these past years I was inwardly hurt when in revival meetings I would witness people being pleaded with and begged to serve God. I experienced the same hurt when people would give a little

26

money into the offering with the attitude that they were honoring God by doing so. Too often people offer to serve God with the attitude that they are being good to God. Even some Christians have forfeited their position or office in the world, they thinking that by doing so they would be uplifting God or giving or showing honor to Him. But I would say here that such "service" is blindness, foolishness and spiritual darkness!

Should God call you to serve Him as priest, you ought to humbly thank Him, for this is your greatest glory. For in so doing, God has highly exalted you. Yet God does not do so because you have something in the world to give Him. Rather, His calling you to serve Him means that He is willing to accept you, and this becomes your glory. For people such as we to be able to serve God is indeed a great honor; it is nothing less than God's grace! And this is truly the gospel. The gospel is not only that the Lord Jesus has saved me but is also the fact that people such as we are granted the opportunity to serve God today. Such is the gospel of grace; in fact, it is the greatest gospel.

Keeping the Priesthood

Hence, in the church today there is no longer a limited priesthood, there is only a general priesthood. The nation of Israel had failed, in that the people of God were separated from the priesthood of God. We must ask God to be merciful to us, that today in the church there will not be any separation between God's people and God's priests. Today in the church God's people are His priests, meaning that where there is a believer, there is a priest—that where there are many brethren, there must be precisely that many priests. Everyone in the church goes before God to offer up spiritual sacrifice, the sacrifice of praise. Everyone in the church goes before God to manage spiritual affairs. This thus means that there is no such thing as a selective ministry in the church but that each and every member in the body of Christ goes before God to serve Him. If this is not so, then this is not the church in reality.

Today if the priesthood is not universal in scope, we must acknowledge that there is no church. In Old Testament times the nation of Israel had failed; the church as the New Testament counterpart should not fail. During these past two thousand years of church history the people have been separated from the priesthood many times. Instead of the people and priests being one and the same in the church, sad to say that there has too often arisen an intermediate class standing between God and His people. This is nothing but the doctrine and practice of the Nicolaitans (Revelation 2:6, 15).

I hope brothers and sisters would already have seen that no intermediate class should ever arise in the church. You cannot accept or tolerate such a division. You must discern what the church truly is. A church is that in which every child of God is a priest. This is therefore to say that we do not ask one or a few people to manage spiritual affairs for us. That would be to say that God will use those few and only those few to speak to us, and through them to manage spiritual matters of the church before God. To have such an intermediate class cannot be accepted by the church as her governing principle.

Please be clear that we have no quarrel with the denominations. For this is not a matter of approval, but a matter having to do with the content of Christianity. Let us be aware of the fact that there is the problem in the church today of an intermediate class of servants, which is that there are only some people who are serving God while the rest of the brethren are simply church members. Only those few are serving God whereas all others are merely members of the church. Whenever members wish to approach God, they must go through those few. In the many church organizations or denominations there is present that intermediate class of which we have spoken. But we cannot accept such a class of servants, for there has been given to the church God's grace which we must not cast aside as did the children of Israel.

Now the way to eliminate this practice of an intermediate class is for all of us to be of that class. You and I need only to kneel before God and say, "Lord, I wish to serve You, I am willing to be Your priest."

This intermediate class is worldly in nature; it comes from the flesh. It is idol worship and comes from loving the world. If from the beginning all the children of God could resist the world and refuse to worship idols, they could offer thanks to God by saying, "Henceforth we live in the world solely for the purpose of serving God." And thus that intermediate class would quite naturally disappear and be abolished. If all the brethren would come to see that their sole profession in life is to serve God, then that intermediate class would automatically be terminated.

Hence, I would hope that you could see this, and that from the very beginning of this new way among us you do not allow this intermediate class to exist. Only through defeat and failure on our part do we allow this intermediate class to exist. It is because God's people must take care of their own business that they let a few in the church take care of spiritual affairs. The most which people do in this regard is to give some money to those who serve God. It seems that each of them is content to do nothing by way of service but to give some money and go about doing his or her own thing. It seems that they all have nothing to do in serving God except that one thing. They may ask themselves, "How can I be a good Christian?" And their response is that they take a little time out to "go to church" and while there give a little money. Thus they make a separation or division between those few serving God and the generality of God's people. Today if we open our hearts we shall come to see that to be Christian is to lay everything at Jesus' feet. In short, to be a Christian is to be a priest.

The Recovery of Priesthood

Let us understand that the departure from the truth perpetrated in the past by the nation of Israel has been the very same departure from that truth perpetrated by the church during these past two thousand years since Pentecost. From the time of the Lord's physical departure from the world till the time covered by the content of the book of Revelation and beyond, all the children of God are to be the priests of God. To be God's children is to be God's priests. Please be clear that there was no problem which arose in this regard from the first through the third century A.D. Though there were isolated instances of some of God's children individually not being priests, there were no instances in a *group* sense wherein God's children were not priests. There was no problem of any serious consequence during this first three-centuries period.

Not till the day when Rome accepted Christianity did the multitudes of people throughout the known world of that day come into the church. There were certain benefits which accrued to those multitudes of believers, because they would now belong to the same group and possess the same religious identity with the Emperor. Formerly, what was Caesar's remained as Caesar's and what was God's remained as God's (Matthew 22:21). This truly was a great victory for Christianity because Emperor Constantine had also believed in the Lord. From that time onward (that is, from 313 A.D. onward), the church would undergo a great change. The original command of the Lord Jesus was that whatever was Caesar's was to be given to Caesar and whatever was God's was to be given to God. Now, however, both Caesar's and God's things were to be given to God. This was indeed a great victory for Christianity.

From the time that Constantine believed the Lord the church had begun to experience a tremendous change. Whereas many now began believing the Lord, it having become fashionable to do so, formerly, Rome had persecuted those of the Christian faith on ten different occasions, with tens of thousands of Christians having been killed in the process. By the time, however, of Constantine, believing in the Lord Jesus meant that a person doing so would automatically become a fellow believer with the Emperor himself. And hence, many people ended up joining the church. Yet, though the believers greatly increased in number, the priests in the church did not. While it was easily possible *to become Christians* during this great change, it was wellnigh impossible for many *to serve God.*

Hence, it could be said that from the fourth century forward the church underwent a drastic change. Many indeed believed and joined the church, but servant-priests to God they did not become. Instead, they pleased the worldly authority of that day and had no thought to serve God. At most they were saved, yet because of their worldly outlook on life it was impossible for them to serve God. So naturally, some spiritual ones among them would rise up to manage the church's affairs. Accordingly, the attitude of the rest of the believers was such that to those spiritual ones in the church they said: "All right, you can serve God, for we are secular people in the church." And hence, we find that from the fourth century onward, there were proportionally only a few who conducted their lives in service to God, whereas the great majority did not.

At the time of the apostles during the first century, each and every one of the believers served God. But commencing with the fourth century most believers ended up conveying the thought that though they were indeed God's people, they would remain in the world and pursue their own affairs and maintain their positions and careers in society. Yes, they would sometimes give some money and conduct themselves as Christians in that manner but they would let those who were spiritual take care of the church's spiritual affairs. As a matter of fact, just as the Israelites had done in worshiping the golden calf idol, which ushered in an intermediate class of Levitical priests, so the people of God's church—from the time of Constantine onward—saw the emergence of her own intermediate class who stood between God and His people. Yes, many multitudes would become God's people in the church of

Christ by having believed in the Lord Jesus, but they did not simultaneously become God's priests who would serve Him.

Today in the Church of Rome the Fathers are also called priests. In the Roman Church here in China they are also called priests. Some national churches also call their leaders priests after the way of the Roman Church. In those same churches those who manage secular affairs are called people, and those who manage spiritual matters are called priests. As was the case in Constantine's day and thereafter, we find that once again priests and people are being separated into two distinct classes in the church.

I pray that brothers and sisters would clearly see one very important fact, which is, that in these last days God wishes to accomplish a work of recovery. I believe that in these last days God will bring all His people to the place of recovery. What needs basically to be recovered is none else but that the members of the entire body of Christ will be priests. And that even during the coming kingdom age, they shall still be priests.

The Priestly Service

So I hope the brethren can clearly see that once anyone and everyone becomes a Christian that one is likewise a priest. Let us not expect some other people in the church to be our priests. You and I ourselves are priests. There is to be no intermediate class in our midst. No one is to take care of spiritual things for us. All the brothers and sisters are to be preaching the gospel. All are to be serving. Christian priesthood is universal in scope. By this we come to discern the true church of God. If in this new way among us the practice of universal priesthood should become less prevailing, then we will have departed from one of the foundational truths concerning the church. If so, we shall have failed to walk well.

For us who are poor, weak and blind, we are nonetheless being made priests by God. And such is our glory. According to the Old Testament, those who were either poor, weak or blind

32

could not be priests. This was because all such disabled people were not allowed to be priests (Leviticus 21:16-23). Today, however, such people as we are can be priests, for God has called us priests! (see again Revelation 5:9-10) I have previously said that I will obey and walk on my knees and declare: "Lord, I am glad to serve You; indeed, I am happy to be Your servant. Allowing me to come before You means that You are uplifting me."

May I tell you, brethren, that to be God's priest means a drawing near to Him. To be God's priest is to have no distance from Him. To be His priest means that I can directly approach Him. To be God's priest means that I do not need to wait for another to be my priest. To be God's priest is to be able to touch Him directly. If one day meetings in every locality have all the brethren serving, that will be the kingdom of God in reality. That will be the priestly nation of God, for all His people are serving. I think this is a most glorious circumstance.

I will also observe that in that day all idols will be eliminated from our midst. We are willing to pay whatever cost involved. For let us recall that the Levites paid an incredibly heavy cost and were found faithful at Sinai, disregarding their own feelings and emotional ties. Such people as they were could be priests to God.

Brothers and sisters, we must more clearly understand what is true priestly ministry, and more clearly understand how in the Old Testament period God treated the priests. God allows you to come willingly forward, as did the tribe of Levi in the day of the golden calf incident. He does not want you to die. Let me tell you that this is something tremendous. Moreover, the priests alone could eat the shewbread. They alone could approach the altar. Only the priests could enter the holy place. Only the priests could offer sacrifices. Anybody else who entered would be struck dead. Hence, let us see that God's acceptance is the foundation of priesthood. Today God is willing to accept us; should we not therefore enter today? Formerly, anyone other than the Levitical priests who might enter would die. Today, however, God has declared: "You all who are My people may come in!" Is it not strange if we do not enter in today? Let us acknowledge before God that He has given us the greatest grace in allowing us to serve Him. All who know God will say that it is more wonderful to be able to serve than even to be saved. The dogs (that is, the Gentiles) might eat the crumbs tossed *under* the table (cf. Mark 7:27-28), but they could not serve the Master *at* the table. To be saved is comparatively simple, but to serve is even more wonderful for all God's people. It is therefore foolish if we do not appreciate such grace and enter upon God's priesthood.

Chapter Three

The Universal Priesthood of Believers

And made us a kingdom, priests to his God and
Father: to him be the glory and the might to the ages
of ages. Amen.

Revelation 1:6

For today's message we need to see what the church is. At
this time in our spiritual history together I believe our light is
very clear. The church is that in which all the believers become
priests. The recovery of such truth has been explained and
taught for over a hundred years. Such has been the case from
1828 till now, a period of a hundred and twenty years.[*] May our
eyes be opened that we may see that the nature of Christian
priesthood is universal. Sadly, even to this day, it is still not
known or acknowledged by all believers. Moreover, the truth
concerning the church as the body of Christ had also been
recovered for a hundred years and more: some of God's people
have especially seen its spiritual value. However, for many
others in the church today it is possible that the truth concerning
the body of Christ has remained merely a teaching, it is yet far
from constituting the life of the church in practice.

Hence we must ask God to open our eyes that we may
know what the body of Christ is. To be that body means that
every member of it is functioning. None of its members is to be
non-functioning. Which is to say, that none of those who belong
to the Lord is exempt from being a serving priest. All the

---

[*] The year 1828 marked the beginning of the so-called Brethren movement
in church history.—*Publishers*

members of the body of Christ are functioning, every one of them is a serving priest.

At this time when the specially called brethren among us go out, they need to encourage the changing of the minds of brothers and sisters elsewhere. Formerly, our thought and concern had been in knowing how many in the church were serving. Today, though, the understanding of our minds must be to see and acknowledge the Biblical truth that the entire church is to be serving. Today we who acknowledge this truth must repeatedly present and share it until in our own day all other brethren equally understand this truth. Please realize that unless the entire church is serving, there is actually no church at all. The members of the entire church of Christ are to rise up and serve. Then we shall be able to say that in this particular area of church life we have matured into becoming a body of Christ in both truth and practice. It must become the case that wherever any believer in Christ is located, that one must have been able to find a local church whose understanding and practice of this truth exist.

But I do not expect you to go about abolishing Sunday preaching and change church practice in this regard all at once. It has to be undertaken and implemented gradually. I do not know if you yourselves gathered here have this vision. If one day the mentality of the children of God is no longer that of today regarding the church's Sunday worship meeting, if they are able to do without hearing messages but are accepting of what God has revealed in the Bible concerning how the entire church herself is to be engaged in service—by which I mean that if on Sunday morning there is the performing of service to people by the entire priesthood of believers—and if, further, the Sunday evening meeting could see the service to God as again being done by the whole church, then I will happily tell you how good that would be.

When out of habit we arise on Sunday morning to gather for worship, it should not matter whether or not we meet. As a matter of fact, we could preach the gospel on some other occasions during the week; for when we rise up on Sunday morning, that can be the time for us as the entire church to go out to reach other people, because each and every one of us ought to be serving. On Sunday evening, however, we can all serve God by offering up our sacrifices of praise and thanksgiving. Only by our doing our service to God by this way can it be rightly said that we are truly a local church according to God's word.

If, immediately after having been saved, each and all of us had had this way in mind about saving others and working to lead them forward in the faith—if, I say, we all had done so according to the above description or something similar to it, then I believe we would have truly witnessed the church as God would want to see her.

Let us suppose, for instance, that immediately after being saved you say to others in the church, "I want to see others saved; so I will bring this one and that one to the church's gospel meeting." That brother or sister thus becomes a worker. He or she is one who bears witness to the truth of the universal priesthood of all believers. I wonder if you have seen this way. We must all work to that extent before we can look upon ourselves as being a local church before God. May I speak frankly, that people in the church, because they belong to God, are right, but their condition or state or practice in the way they do things as members in the church is not right, for too many are too passive.

Therefore, I firmly believe that as you leave this upcoming training mission, you need to change your way of working. You need to have a center or working principle upon which you focus your attention and apply yourselves to accomplish. Indeed, according to Ephesians 4:11-12, you will need to change the very nature of your work: you workers, in your work for the Lord, should lead the people in the church to do the work, not that you should work for them. What, then, shall be your working principle?—answer: to save people; and this thus becomes your work.

From now on, let there not be any difference between workers and the rest of the church brethren. Even though the workers may be spiritually stronger than the brethren, nevertheless, as far as work is concerned, there is to be no difference between the two, since they are all expected to be working together. Only then shall we be able to understand the New Testament concept of the body of Christ. For the entire New Testament bears witness to the truth that all the children of God are deemed to be coworkers for they are all working. The only difference lies in you who have been called to spend your entire time and strength in church work, having been commissioned by God to work all the time and everywhere. I especially hope we can all now understand. Let me tell you that if you are spiritually strong, you will press forward till all unnecessary or incorrect or unbiblical traditions fall away.

Supplying God's Word within Various Contexts

Before proceeding further in our discussion on the way of the church, I would like to spend our remaining time today considering together the supplying of God's word on various occasions in our corporate life as the church.

With regard first to the supply of His word for beginners, we have prepared fifty-two subjects or lessons. Please bear in mind that if we are strong in preaching the gospel, there will be more people getting saved. And the more who are saved will mean that the church will need to do more for them. Thus our intention will be to present one lesson per week to new believers. Every week, either on Thursday or Friday evening, we will gather new believers for them to receive one lesson from those fifty-two basic lessons which we have prepared. If so, then after a year's time has passed, all those basic lessons will have been taught, resulting in the fact that new believers in our midst will not be lacking in the word of God.* In this way, after engaging in continued gospel work and having taught the fifty-two basic lessons, I believe we can thereafter easily supply God's word for building up the faith and corporate life of the church. Thus, brethren need not go anywhere else to receive their necessary spiritual food. If we all as God's workers are alive before Him, these new converts to the faith will be living. Otherwise, all such new believers will simply be and remain the Lord's people and nothing further. If, though, we all are alive before God, even the dead will become alive. On the other hand, if we are dead before God, then the living among us will become dead. The Gospel according to John is living, yet it too will become dead if we are dead as His servants before God. But if we are living and serving before Him, then I believe that year after year we can repeat these fifty-two basic lessons for those further beginners in the faith. The lessons' words may be repeated; even so, the Anointing can also repeat itself; and thus spiritual life can also be seen repeated yearly.

Here, then, we need to consider two different church meeting-times together in relation to the matter of gospel outreach and to each other: On Sunday morning, we have a

---

* The reader needs to be aware that all 52 Lessons have been translated and published in English by the present Publishers in the past, and are still in print and available, as follows: one Lesson (Sickness) can be found as part of one lengthy chapter on that subject in Watchman Nee, *The Spiritual Man* (New York: Christian Fellowship Publishers, the 3-vol. Combined Edition, 1977), vol. 3, Part 10, Ch. 2); 3 other Lessons form Part Two of Watchman Nee's *The Spirit of Judgment* (New York: CFP, 1984); and the remaining 48 Lessons have been rearranged and variously grouped together into six separate volumes and published under the general title of The Basic Lesson Series (New York: CFP, 1972-75). These six individual volume titles in this Series are entitled: *A Living Sacrifice* (1972), *The Good Confession* (1973), *Assembling Together* (1973), *Not I, But Christ* (1974), *Do All to the Glory of God* (1974), and *Love One Another* (1975).—*Publishers*

gospel meeting. Let us not be afraid of not having the traditional Sunday message as though something vital is missing. We must pay attention to preach the gospel at this time and to save souls. And then, for those new believers who come into the church, we provide them on Thursday or Friday evening with one of the weekly fifty-two basic lessons to lead them on in the faith. Hence, on Sunday morning the supply of God's word is in the form of the gospel, while on Thursday or Friday evening, God's word is presented as a way to build up the new believers in Christ.

Now with respect to the supply of God's word in the manner of I Corinthians 14, some of you may comment and inquire along this line of thought: If in a local church there are elderly brothers in the midst along with many other brothers and sisters, how should we supply the latter with the word of God? I would tell you and them that that can be what the Saturday evening gathering is for—it is a time for the exercise of various gifts according to what I Corinthians 14 calls for: some present have a word from the Scriptures, some have a revelation, some have spiritual songs, some have prayers, etc., etc. So, today, if some brethren feel that it is not enough to supply God's word only at the beginners' meetings on Thursday/Friday evening and Sunday morning, then on Saturday evening let those brothers in service conduct a strong and edifying meeting.

So my thought is, let us preach the gospel on Sunday morning, let us set aside Thursday or Friday evening for teaching beginners the basic lessons, and perhaps also on Saturday evening there can be a I Corinthians 14-like meeting. Thus, you are able to supply all of God's children in the church with the word of the Lord. And hence, the meeting on Saturday evening has the possibility of becoming very lively, unlike the deadness of our currently conducted Sunday morning services. As we all know, the Sunday message currently delivered is usually undertaken by one worker, which can present quite a difficult situation; for regardless whether or not that worker has an anointed word, he nonetheless must stand up and speak. It would appear to be the thinking among us today that if we do not provide a traditionally-expected Sunday morning message, brothers and sisters would probably leave us. If that be the case, then it would seem as though we are using the Sunday morning message as a way to keep the brothers and sisters from leaving. It is my hope, therefore, that henceforth what will retain them is not Sunday messages as currently being delivered; instead, I hope it will be the preaching of the gospel on Sunday morning. If so, then everybody will be engaged in edifying others, everyone will be preaching the gospel, and serving up helpful gospel-related words. And hence, this can be what will keep brethren in the church. Let us cause all the brethren to labor together in the gospel till it becomes habitual. We must give every believer in the church a chance to work and serve till it becomes a personal habit of theirs. And thus shall the church be well established and built up.

Let us, for example, say that in the local church of a certain locality there is held each week a gospel meeting on Sunday morning. The responsible brothers there will work out an arrangement before God whereby each of them will be responsible for a term or period of time—say, for a month or for two months—in preaching a gospel message. The entire church is there preaching the gospel together: all are engaged in serving those people present who are unbelievers. And when those unbelievers are saved, bring them to the Thursday or Friday evening meeting for hearing one of the fifty-two basic lessons. Upon their attending those weekly evening meetings for a whole year, they will have received all the basic lessons for growth in faith. Then those among them who have a word from the Scriptures, they can rise up at the Saturday evening meeting and speak an edifying word.

Currently, in many places the Saturday evening meeting is not strong. This is because many who have gifts or have responsibilities are passive on Saturday evening. Unless they are burdened, as they often are at the Sunday morning meeting, they tend to rest at the Saturday evening meeting. Since they are resting and have no burden, how can that Saturday meeting be strong? How is it that everybody in responsibility is passive? Consequently, it should be understood that the Saturday evening I Corinthians 14-type meeting is not to be the kind of meeting where all brothers and sisters present are responsible. Please realize that in such a gathering of the church it is wrong for either one person to be responsible or for all to be responsible.

Now I will share with you here what responsible brothers should do at a Saturday evening meeting. As is the case with all other church meetings, the responsible brothers should arrive at least half an hour earlier to have prayers. That should be the practice with respect to the gospel meeting as well as to the meeting for new believers. It should also be the case with the prayer meeting as well as with the breaking-of-bread gathering. Hence, let me repeat that in reference to the Saturday evening gathering, all the church's responsible brothers should arrive half an hour—or at least fifteen minutes—earlier so that they may have some prayers and for making preparation. In fact, I would even suggest that especially in regard to the Saturday evening meeting, responsible brethren need more time: if they need to arrive fifteen minutes earlier in the case of ordinary meetings, then for this Saturday meeting they should be present a half an hour earlier. They should have an understanding among themselves to come together for half an hour of prayer. Whereas the other church brethren may come unprepared, the responsible brothers must gain confidence before God ahead of the meeting. No responsible brother should conduct himself carelessly in this regard when approaching the time of meeting; to the contrary, all responsible brothers must make themselves ready before God in advance of the meeting.

Allow me to speak frankly that in many local churches there are many brethren present on Saturday evening who want to speak. Because of this, you responsible brothers should pray for them that they will not occupy the total preaching. Indeed, you should pray that only those who have a burden before God will stand up and contribute. Thus, you must pray that the Saturday evening meetings will be spiritually strong and impressive.

Especially for the Saturday evening meeting, those brothers in responsibility should find out who among themselves have special burdens for that evening. Brothers in responsibility should bear the ministry of God's word more. Even though, generally speaking, elders are not primarily gifted or called of God for the preaching of His word, nevertheless, we must acknowledge that they should be able to exhort (cf. I Timothy 3:2). So when those who are able to share are together, they should seek out who among them especially have a burden for that evening. All those bearing responsibility in the church must have burden, but when they are together in advance of the start of the meeting, they need to find out who is especially burdened for that night. Everyone among the eldership has burden, but not all of them have a special burden. They should seek out among themselves as to whether there is any special word from the Lord for that meeting.

Accordingly, at least the responsible brothers are not to be passive. Please be advised, therefore, that if the responsible brothers are passive, the entire body of Christ present will be inactive that evening.

I have often wondered why it is that if there are three to five responsible brothers who have something from God's word, they nonetheless permit the Saturday evening meeting to be open to all present to contribute something, thus allowing other brothers to speak who really have no burden. Then, when afterwards, with the meeting having looked bad, they shake their heads and admit that the meeting was bad. Candidly speaking, I would say that if the mouth did not speak but the nose was allowed to speak, no wonder the sound ended up not being right! On many occasions that was the trouble. Those same responsible brothers did nothing to curb such behavior at that Saturday evening I Corinthians 14-type meeting. They did nothing but criticize afterwards. How strange and puzzling that was!

Let me speak frankly here that the condition of the church today is unlike what is called for by the New Testament. Hence, we need to change our mentality and approach to our various church meetings. God is looking for the way of recovery among us, so we must walk in the way of recovery. We need to bring all the brothers and sisters to the point of them all working and serving. They all are to serve sinners, they all are to serve new believers, and they all are to serve one another. And in particular, they all are to be ready to serve one another—if burdened—with God's word according to I Corinthians 14.

If there is the need for spiritual supply, we need to be able to send out as many brothers who can work. Instead of their being kept in one locality, let them move around. They may stay in one place for three to five days, and then they can move on to another locality.

I believe by so doing, the condition of every locality will be similar and new people coming into the local churches will be greatly multiplied. If the entire church in every locality is busy preaching, that will be a tremendous and most positive development.

Chapter Four

The Levitical Service

Bring the tribe of Levi near, and present them
before Aaron the priest, that they may minister unto
him; and they shall keep his charge, and the charge of
the whole assembly, before the tent of meeting, to do
the service of the tabernacle.

Numbers 3:6-7

Concerning Levitical service, we do not need to say much,
for it is very simple. In Old Testament times the Levitical
service was different from priestly service. Priests were to serve
God as well as to serve the tabernacle, whereas the Levites were
to serve the priests as a way of helping them to fulfill their
service to God and the tabernacle. In other words, priestly
service back then represented spiritual service, whereas that of
the Levites was serving the secular or business side of things:
they were responsible to wash the blood from off the bullock,
take away all refuse, strip the skin of the sacrifice, and carry
forward the tabernacle with its many parts. Whenever God's
pillar of cloud began to be lifted, thus signaling that the
tabernacle was to be broken up for being transported forward,
the Levites would carry the furnishings, holy objects, and the
various other items which belonged to the tabernacle (Numbers
3, 18:1-4; I Chronicles 23:24-32). Such, then, were the different
kinds of service for which the Levites were responsible.

In the World, Yet Not of the World

From this description, therefore, we can see that though the
work of the Levites was not spiritual, it was nonetheless related
to the spiritual. Though it was associated, as it were, with the

world, yet, back then, it was not of the world but was of the tabernacle and later of the temple. And hence, according to the Bible, it can be said that in the New Testament church of today the service of the deacons (e.g., Acts 6:1-6, I Timothy 3:8-13) has the character of the service of the Old Testament Levites.

There being deacons in the church, the nature of their work can be likened to the nature of the work of the Levites. They take care of the physical, business or secular side of service in the church.

All Must Learn to Serve

All the brothers and sisters should be involved in the taking care of the secular or physical side of church affairs. They should all be at work in doing such tasks as the cleaning of the meeting place and its environs, as well as of its benches and mosquito nets[*]. Caring for the poor should also be their work. Transporting visiting brothers and sisters is also Levitical-type work. You can see before God that such Levitical sorts of services are quite numerous. Many works in the church office can also be classified as works of the Levites. While a person is serving God, he or she has, on the one hand, the work of a priest and, on the other hand, the work of a Levite. He or she must do both. He or she must serve a part in spiritual service as well as a part in the church's secular or business side of service. Please recall that Stephen and some other deacons took care of distributing food (Acts 6:1-6). Such is the work of the deacons who are the New Testament counterparts to the Old Testament Levites. Recall, too, how the disciples of Jesus went forward to distribute bread, and afterwards they gathered up twelve and, on a later occasion, seven baskets of bread fragments (Matthew 14:20, 15:37). These are examples of deacons' jobs. For Judas Iscariot to have taken charge of the disciples' money bag was also a deacon's job (John 13:29). From the place of Jacob's well

---

[*] Having mosquito nets to manage was a normal situation for this time period in China.—*Publishers*

in Samaria Jesus sent forth His disciples to buy bread, and that too can be defined as a deacon's job (John 4:8, 33). All these were major examples of the work of Jesus' followers in His day. All in the church of Christ today must learn to serve in these ways.

Helping Out in Homes

Here I would like to mention an idea to which I hope brothers and sisters would pay special attention. Whereas many brothers and some sisters have much leisure time on their hands, many other sisters at home have no leisure at all, for they must cook, do house work, as well as take care of children. In terms of Levitical service, therefore, we ought to arrange to have people go to their homes and help out. For example, responsible brethren could tell those sisters in their homes that there are among the church brethren two or three sisters who could help them to wash their clothes for two hours. Such could be another form of Levitical-type service. At the time of the early church the Hellenistic widows were overlooked in the matter of their lack of food supply, and so there were murmurings (Acts 6:1). Such was the church situation at that time. Although this was not a spiritual matter as such, nevertheless, the need had to be taken care of, and it eventually was (vv. 2-6).

Twelve Forms of Physical Service

Here are a number of physical works which can be done. 1. Cleaning work. 2. Taking care of the meeting place and showing hospitality. 3. Some brothers and sisters need to take care of the Lord's Table and the arrangements for baptism: that is to say, the bread and the cup need people to take care of such; people are also needed who are trained for handling certain aspects of baptisms—the arranging of clothing of those being baptized, for instance, can be one of their jobs. 4. Care for the unbelieving poor or when there is a flood or a fire: the church should rise up to care for them. 5. The poor among the saints

47

need to be supplied with the barest essentials. 6. Brethren who go out and come in need to be sent forth and/or met, and done so in a proper manner. 7. Several brethren should take care of the church's bookkeeping. 8. Some church members should be given responsibility in taking care of food arrangements. 9. Other brethren should work in the church office. 10. Still others can take care of cars if there is such a need. 11. Still other brethren could take care of correspondence. And 12. Some could render help in the houses of the poor brothers and sisters by assisting them in various home tasks like washing dishes and clothing and doing mending, etc.

I sincerely hope that every brother and sister would take up the burden of assisting in various physical or business-type church affairs. Let there not be some who work and some who do not work, for undertaking these various kinds of church affairs should be carried out by all. It would also be good for brothers or sisters who have leisure time to help in the household chores of brothers and sisters coming from outside. Every week for an hour or two some brethren ought to go to the homes of those believers who now and then come from outside and help them in various time-consuming or difficult tasks. Moreover, it would be good for those wealthy sisters to go to the less fortunate brothers' or sisters' houses to do washing or mending. There should not be special people to do such tasks while those wealthy sisters do nothing. Instead, the latter ought to be willing to go to those less fortunate families with difficulties and assist them in household chores and help them out financially with their lunches and other meals. All such works of service are Christ-like in character.

The Principle Is for All to Serve

So much for those church affairs which are of a physical or business character. The principle is clear. All brothers and sisters must be involved in practical service as well as in spiritual service. Whether one serves more or less, all must be involved and serve as much as possible. May I again say, brethren, that you yourselves must see this, and thus your responsibility shall be great and you shall be quite busy. In this way, however, the church shall have a solid foundation. Moreover, people will know that there is a local church in their midst by the fact that we all are involved in physical matters as well as in spiritual ones.

Causing All with One Talent to Work

Here I would like to speak, in particular, to responsible brothers. You have a natural tendency—even a habit—of loving to use those people who have been gifted with two or more talents. Church history proves it. Those brethren possessing five talents know how to use the two-talent ones. Indeed, they do not need to be urged to do so. But the question is, How to engage and use the one-talent folk? The latter, for instance, may utter a few helpful words from Scripture on occasion but then cease to speak further, whereas the two-talent believers are most accessible and available all the time. They all have some ability and know how to do things; and so, they do not bury their talents. Yet, if you only use those with two talents but are not able to engage the one-talent people to serve, you have totally failed.

What is a true New Testament church? Such a church is one in which all the one-talent brethren will come forward and perform service in those practical and physical matters as well as in spiritual ones. You responsible brothers must not shake your head and declare that this or that person is useless. If so, you are totally defeated and the church is finished. If you consider this or that believer inaccessible and therefore useless, then that person shall remain inaccessible and useless; but be reminded that the Lord has given that one a talent and has instructed that one-talent person to serve (cf. Matthew 25:24-27). Though the Lord can use such ones, it becomes clear that you cannot, and this thus proves that you are not fit to be a leader. Consequently, you who are responsible brothers must bring in even those apparently useless one-talent brethren. Such, then, is a most important work. You should not only use those *obviously* usable multi-talented brothers and sisters, you should make use of the seemingly useless single-talented brothers and sisters as well.

As we have just now seen from Matthew 25 a basic Biblical principle is that the Lord never gives less than one talent to any of His followers. Therefore, in the house of the Lord not a single servant is without a talent: he or she has at least one. No one can say: "The Lord has not given me anything." Not so! I want all of us to know and acknowledge this one truth—that all the children of God are servants before Him. To be God's children is to be His servants. In other words, to be members of His church automatically means that all such members have been gifted, and hence, all are also to be servants. If we who are responsible in God's church consider anyone not able to be engaged and usable, we do not truly know the grace of God. We must clearly see and understand His grace. When God says that this man or woman is My servant, neither you nor I can stand up and say he or she is not. Too often today, if any of you have been placed in a position of sharing in the church's responsibility, you may have the tendency or habit of selecting only those with two or more talents as servants. Yet God says that all members of the body of Christ are servants. If God has declared that all are His servants, then we should and must let all of them serve.

I must assert here, brothers and sisters, that whether or not our work has an effective way today depends on how we look at our work: do we rely only on a few especially gifted in the church or do we look upon all members as being God's servants who need to take part in the work and service of the church? The question before us all is therefore this: Does the *entire* church serve, or just a few? This is the essential question. If this question is not addressed—and addressed correctly according to God's word—then nothing along this line can be accomplished.

The Body of Christ vs the Pastor System

The body of Christ is not merely a doctrine, it is also a living reality. We need to recognize this and put it into practice. Only when every member is working do we have the body of Christ in reality.

Today the solution to this problem is in our hands. Unfortunately, we have adopted the Father system of the Roman Church and the pastor system of the Reformed Church. Unless we are careful we will end up establishing an intermediate system in which a few members take care of all the works of service. It is in vain to simply *preach* the body of Christ. It must also be *practiced.* Let us not be afraid if such a practice proves to be workable. We can put our trust in the living reality of the body of Christ. May we allow and engage all her members to rise up and serve.

God Has Gone before Us

If I am not mistaken, I sense that our time for putting into practice the reality of the body of Christ has arrived. The letters I have received and the news I have heard—all demonstrate that it is time for the entire body of Christ to be involved in serving. God has gone ahead of us and we must follow after. I do not expect or desire to see a brother or a few brothers going forward to work and serve on behalf of all the other brethren; rather, I expect and desire a brother to lead eight or ten others to serve, and after a while to use sixty or eighty or even a hundred others to serve. And when any of us might visit that church again, I would hope to see a thousand or two who are serving in that expression of the body of Christ. I tell you that this is absolutely correct Biblically. If any of you engage the five-talent brethren in place of the two-talent ones or engage the two-talent brethren in place of the one-talent ones, you are not God's servant;

51

instead, you must cause the five-talent ones, the two-talent ones, and the one-talent ones—all of them—to serve. You are to cause those whom you might consider as unavailable and useless to rise up and serve. Only then shall you see the glorious church.

I do not expect or desire to see only three or five gifted brethren engaged in preaching; in fact, I do not admire those few special people; I would prefer to see all the one-talent folk serving in various ways, including even serving in the work of preaching. The Lord *may* give us more Pauls or more Peters, but thus far He has not done that. The world is full of the one-talent folk. Where and when will you place those of them who shall have become believers?

Authority Solves the Flesh Problem

We are not afraid of the activities of the one-talent believers' flesh. There are two ways for the church to be established and built up. One is the way of authority and the other is that of gift. All the one-talent people must come forth in service. They ought to labor in service and bear fruits. But you who are responsible brethren might well say that if the people with one talent serve with their flesh—as may very well be the case—how can we solve the flesh problem? I must first tell you that, indeed, the flesh has to be dealt with; and next, that the solution lies in the exercise of authority, which represents God.

Gift and authority are two different expressions: the one-talent believers will express their gift by using their talent in service, and if they should bring in their flesh, the latter problem can be settled by your exercising God's authority in the matter: you need to say to such a one, "Brother (or Sister), you cannot bring your flesh into your work of service; on the contrary, such an attitude or conduct is not right, and we do not allow the Lord's people to have such an attitude or conduct themselves in that manner." Because of your conveying this to that one, he or she may well return home that same day and refuse to perform any more service. Nevertheless, you must go find that one and say to him/her that he or she as a member of the body of Christ must continue to serve. And even though that person's flesh may still be manifested, you must nonetheless let that one continue to serve. Except that you must convey to that person *again* that bringing in the flesh cannot be tolerated in the church. And thus, we who are responsible ones in the church must use authority with which to deal with the matter of the flesh.

The manifesting of the flesh is a great temptation for the one-talent folk in the church to engage in. Too often the moment they are used by the Lord becomes the very moment that their flesh intrudes into their work of service. In fact, the flesh and the one-talent gift seem to go together. On the one hand, we must resist the flesh; on the other hand, we must also put to use the ones with a one-talent gift. The problem arises today that as we bury the flesh we also bury the one-talent gift (cf. Matthew 25:25), with the result that the church as it should be disappears. No, the flesh continually needs to be dealt with by the exercise of authority while simultaneously the use of those with the one-talent gift must continue to be encouraged. Perhaps those one-talent believers will complain by saying, "What then can we do if on the one hand we are encouraged to serve but on the other hand we are restrained from serving? Moreover, we are told that if we serve in such a way, our flesh may come in, and if we do not serve, we bury our one-talent gift!" We must see to it that those with the one-talent gift must be brought into the service of the church, but the flesh cannot be permitted to come in. If in the church God's authority is exercised—and exercised properly—and all of her talents can be brought in, we shall soon witness on earth a glorious church.

I do not know how much time the Lord has given to us to effect this change in our midst, though I realize that this way has become clear. We must use all our thoughts and strength to help brothers and sisters rise up and serve. And thus, the church shall be built up and matured (Ephesians 4:13b), and then the Lord shall return. May the Lord have mercy on us that we may accordingly do His will.

Chapter Five

The Priestly Service

To him who loves us, and has washed us from our
sins in his blood, and made us a kingdom, priests to
his God and Father: to him be the glory and the might
to the ages of ages. Amen.

Revelation 1:5b-6

As was noted previously, I believe the primary
understanding regarding the principle of priestly service in the
church is that all God's people are priests—none is excepted:
all must serve God. In accordance, therefore, with this
understanding, how should we make sure that all the brothers
and sisters are engaged in priestly service in the local assembly?
In other words, how should we so arrange the spiritual work of
the church in such a way that all the believers—both those who
have believed the Lord for many years and those who have only
newly believed—will take part in spiritual works? In response,
let us spend some time in considering what and how much of
spiritual works in a local assembly should brothers and sisters
be allowed to do.

All Believers Should Do Certain Spiritual Works

As a beginning, we have arranged for some assemblies to
have local brothers and sisters engaged in performing the
following various forms of spiritual service.

First, the preaching of the gospel.

Second, regarding a person who says he or she has been
saved after having heard the gospel, we will visit that one in
order to lead him/her in the right way, informing that one on
how to be a Christian.

Third, visiting the newly-believed. After an outsider has believed in the Lord and been baptized, how should we help that one?

Fourth, there are many needs in the church. Some brethren have family difficulties of various kinds: some are sick, some incur painful developments, sadly some must arrange for funerals, and some experience happy circumstances. All kinds of things happen in families which may need the help of the church. Taken together, we may call all these diverse family circumstances as occasions for special visitation.

Fifth, and finally, there is the need to care for those who travel and render help to those who come to visit. I always feel that this is an important service to be undertaken. When a brother or a sister travels, a letter of recommendation should be given and even care for him or her should be provided afterwards. Also, those brothers or sisters who come to visit likewise need special care shown them.

If we can perform these five different works of spiritual service, we will do well. Let us take up each one in greater detail.

First—Preaching the Gospel

The first of these works of spiritual service calls our attention to the preaching of the gospel. "Do the work of an evangelist" (II Timothy 4:5b) said Paul to Timothy, his son in the faith and a leader in the church of Christ. God has established in the church those who preach the gospel. Even to those who may not be able to preach formally from a platform, the command of the apostle Paul is to do the work of an evangelist. Such a word means that those who can publicly preach will preach the gospel, and those who are not able to so preach are nonetheless exhorted to likewise do the evangelizing work of the gospel. In other words, those who should publicly preach the gospel should so preach, and those who do not so preach should also do the work of evangelism. If God grants you the gift of preaching the gospel, you should do so wholeheartedly in order to bring new believers into the church. If, on the other hand, God has not established you as a preacher of the gospel, even so, you as a child of God should be burdened to engage in gospel work.

This gospel work must be done by all young people like the younger Timothy; and all others in the faith should be involved in gospel work as well.

We who are responsible leaders in the church should encourage all the brothers and sisters to spend time in going out to do the work of evangelizing. Let us never allow them to forget the sinners by our letting only a few do the work of preaching the gospel. Rather, we need to make clear to all brothers and sisters that all brethren in Christ are priests and all must therefore serve God in the various ways of spiritual service. And one of the ways of spiritual service is most certainly that of sharing the gospel with unbelievers. May we give special attention to this when encouraging brothers and sisters in this matter of the universal priesthood of believers.

Second—Showing Care During and After Hearing the Gospel

This service responsibility consists of bringing an unbeliever to the meeting till that one is baptized. You and I need to show all church brethren how great is their responsibility. They must bring people from school, hospital or office to the meeting place on a continuing basis till such ones know the Lord, accept Him, and are baptized. This in summary is the gospel-caring process that should be followed. Here are some details which may be helpful in fulfilling this caring process.

Bring Them to the Gospel Meeting

Each time you care for the sinners you should bring them to the gospel meetings. Do not bring too many people on any one occasion. To ensure better care, bring only three or four unbelievers each time. It is not our intention to make a rule, but two or four is a better number. If from school you could bring in thirty or even fifty young sinners, then you need to ask the responsible brothers in the local church to assign other brothers and sisters to share in such caring responsibility. Otherwise, if you as one church member can only care for four people at a time and yet you could bring forty sinners in to the gospel meeting, then the other thirty-six sinners would be left without personal care. Hence, you should ask the local responsible brothers to assign other brothers and sisters to care for the other thirty-six.

Sit among the Brought-In Sinners

In order to best care for the sinners at the gospel meeting, you should prepare in advance the necessary hymn books and Bibles. In caring for four unbelievers, you can let two sit on your left and two on your right. Two of them seated beside you on each side is the limit, otherwise it will be inefficient. Help them to find the Bible verses and/or the hymn numbers. Do not consider any of the four to be an expert in finding verse or number. They have never been experts in doing so. They have probably never sung a hymn before nor have they probably ever read the Bible. So you must help them in this regard.

If and when at any given moment they do not understand what is being preached, you need to explain it to them in a very low voice so as not to distract others in the audience. In this connection, a brother once went to Japan to preach the gospel in a large meeting. Many unbelievers were present. His first word was, "You all know about the children of Israel having left Egypt." Paget Wilkes—a missionary in Japan— immediately went up to the platform to tell that preaching brother that it would require two hours for him to explain to the unbelievers present who were the Israelites and why they had left Egypt. We should realize that many things concerning the Bible the average sinner does not understand nor is at all acquainted with. Though you caring brethren do not have at your disposal two hours with which to explain something being preached at the gospel meeting, you can perhaps express in one or two sentences what needs to be explained to those unbelievers sitting beside you. But you need to do so in the lowest tone of voice.

Be in Prayer to Help the Preaching

Your greatest assistance in helping the gospel preaching that is occurring from the platform is to be attentive and to pray, and certainly not to criticize. Let all believers present understand that gospel preaching is not a preaching to you and me but to and for the sinner. Much gospel preaching does not go well because the brothers and sisters present do not carefully listen. Please be advised that none of us brethren *under* the platform come to criticize the gospel speaker but to help. The gospel is not being preached to us who already believe but to the sinners present.

Hence, when you sit by the side of the unbelievers, you should silently pray when you sense that the anointed spirit of the preacher has come forth and that the words are strong. At that moment you should quietly pray: "Lord, send this word to people's hearts. Lord, use this word to save this or that person; Lord, use this word to save those two persons there." Perhaps the Lord will save them—one, if you say one; or two, if you say two. If you pray for one, the Lord will give you one. If you pray for four, the Lord will give you four. You use prayer to strengthen the word being preached and you pray for the four persons who may be sitting by your side. This is what all the brethren in the church need to be responsible for doing.

At the Time of Pulling in the Net

There must be the time of pulling the net in at each gospel meeting. Casting forth the net is one thing, pulling in the net is an entirely different matter. After the preaching is finished, it is time to pull the net in by asking people to raise their hands in response. At that time, you should render some help. There are many different ways to help at this moment. For some, you may have to nudge them to get in; in that case, you need to pray on the one hand and strongly persuade them on the other hand. If you recognize that it is pride which stands in the way of their believing, you will advise them to be humble. If the reason why this person or that person does not stand up or raise their hands is because of their love of the world, you may quietly say to them such words as this: "What good is the world to you; why wait for another time? Do not wait if you feel the time is ripe."

Waiting Four Months for Gospel Harvest: a Wrong Concept

There is a very important point to be observed in relation to the preaching of the gospel: Do not wait for four months. Many have this wrong concept of waiting for four months before harvesting new believers. But the word of the Lord Jesus to us is that we are not to wait four months in harvesting fresh converts. His word is truly clear and wonderful. He said to His disciples: "Do you not say that there are four months yet before the harvest? But I tell you, the time of the harvest is already here: it can be reaped" (see John 4:35). Hence, the timing of the gospel harvest is far different and much sooner than human estimate would conclude. May we not be so foolish as to think that there will be four months after preaching the gospel before any harvest can occur. The Lord Jesus has said, in so many words, that the time of harvest of souls is always present—that we may harvest lost souls for Him whenever we scatter the gospel seed.

Accordingly, at the time of preaching the gospel, and as you are sitting beside unbelievers, and regardless whether you sense the time of harvest is ripe or not, you should not be bound in the least by the four-months notion. For is it not true that on the one hand there are some souls whom you think are unready, and yet, they believe at once; whereas there are other souls whom you consider as being ready, but it turns out that they may not be so. Therefore, as to these latter sinners, we must encourage them anyhow to accept the Lord today and be harvested for Him.

Let us bear in mind that this matter of lost souls being ready or not is not our responsibility. It depends on the enlightenment of the Holy Spirit. I know at least a few people who pretended to believe but in the end they truly got saved. So, whether ready or not, all unbelievers at the gospel meeting must be encouraged to receive the Lord and be harvested.

All Are Priests

Unless all church members are involved, this gospel work cannot be done. Let us responsible ones help all the brothers and sisters to realize that they are all priests, and hence, every single one of them must be involved. Then we shall immediately see that the gospel meeting will be strong. This is a matter of the entire church preaching the gospel. May we be able to say emphatically that it is the church as a whole that is preaching the gospel. All the brothers and sisters are working. All are priests, therefore, all serve. I say again that unless this be true, there is no church.

As Many As Are Priests, So Are God's People

May I repeat something here which I have said for years and which I deeply sense I should again express today. And it is simply this: "As they are who serve, so are there many in the church; as many as are priests, so are God's people." Let us not turn this statement around and say that "as many are God's people, so are the priests." No, that is wrong to say. Instead, the correct way to say it is: "As many as are priests, so are God's people." Or to put it another way: "As much are those who serve, so are the people of God."

61

When I was in England, I met a brother who in spiritual matters was quite knowledgeable. One day he observed to me that many members of the body of Christ were functional while many other members had no function. I said in reply that according to the Bible all are functional members; and I added that if there was any member of the body of Christ not functional, he or she was probably an appendix. To which that brother broke into great laughter. Many Christians today actually believe that some members have functions while some other members do not. May I ask those who believe this to show me the place where some members are not functional—where are they to be found? For the only non-functional member in the body of Christ must be regarded as an appendix. So I am moved to say today that as many as are functional members, so all are the members of Christ's body.

We Are a Body of Priests

Concerning the aforesaid matter currently under discussion, our incorrect thought needs to be turned around. We need to see and emphasize today that service is *church* service—that, for example, preaching the gospel is a *church* affair; by which is meant that priesthood includes everyone of us who believe. It cannot be the case that out of a thousand or five thousand who comprise a local church, only a few come forth to serve. We cannot tolerate even *one* non-functioning member. Please realize that if you are a member in the body of Christ, you have a function to exercise. You cannot be without any function, for this is a foundational principle of the church of God. May I tell you frankly, brothers and sisters, that without this being true of us in reality, where is the spirit of the New Testament among us? The Catholic Church has the priestly system. And even the Protestant Church has the pastoral system. Please bear in mind continually that we are not to have either the priestly or the pastor system. Yes, we are a priestly group, but *all* in the body of Christ are priests to God.

Third—Care for New Believers

Meeting for New Believers

After a person has believed and is baptized, we need to bring that one to the weekly meeting set aside for new believers. In this meeting, every week there will be a special Biblical subject being taught.

When someone comes to this meeting for beginners, it should be arranged to have some older believer to take care of each such beginner, helping that one to follow and understand the lesson being taught and learned.

If any new beginners do not attend that meeting, they should immediately be visited to remedy the lack of a particular lesson not having been heard. For those, however, who have attended a given weekly meeting, find out from them if they have understood the lesson that was presented.

We cannot conclude that any of the newly saved have fully understood what has been taught at any given meeting for new believers. We want to be sure they have understood what they have heard. Those who are responsible for new believers must pay special attention to this matter.

Fifty-two Topics Need to Be Taught

All know that we have prepared fifty-two Biblical topics for new believers to hear and learn. In a given year all fifty-two weekly topics from the Bible can be covered. Thus, each of these fifty-two subjects can be presented each week. The older brothers and sisters should be familiar with these subjects. Having themselves put into practice these topics before, they are therefore able to lead the newly-believed ones. Of the fifty-two subjects, much attention should have been paid to those having to do with behavior—all of which need to be put into practice. For this reason, unless you older brethren have done these before, you will not know the condition of these newly-saved brethren. None can force them to do them.

This is not a matter of merely listening to messages—that will not at all do. Hence, on the one hand, let them listen to the messages from the speaker's platform, and on the other hand, let some older brothers or sisters visit them during the week as an aid in helping them to implement the content of these Biblical topics into their daily lives. There are many problems that will arise which cannot be resolved with just one visit paid to them by older brethren; rather, it will require many weekly visits to ensure that the newly-saved ones will have studied the Bible verses or made progress in prayers.

The church as a whole should pay particular attention to these beginners in the faith in order that they may be brought to a good position in their daily walk with the Lord. So the challenge here is a matter of leading, not one of knowing. All the different local churches among us should exert their strength and energy to do this work of service. For this is a spiritual service that is so serious and weighty in importance that it cannot be accomplished in a casual manner.

Fourth—Taking Care of Problems among the Brethren

This Does Not Require Many to Be Involved.

In the several works of service already discussed—preaching the gospel, caring for the gospel listeners, and caring for the newly-believing ones—almost all the members of Christ's body need to be involved. Not so, however, for taking care of problems which arise among the local church brethren. Only a few brothers and sisters who have more spiritual weight should be involved. Indeed, in a given local church, I would think that it requires only four or five of such maturer brethren to meet this particular need.

When any brothers and/or sisters have difficulties, these few maturer church brethren can help. Let them rejoice with those who have happy circumstances so as to help them in praising God and in praying with them to have a right attitude. However, for those who have met with sorrowful circumstances, such as someone close having died, let those with spiritual weight share in such sorrow with these grieving brethren in the church, helping them and praying with them. Or if there are family quarrels, those mature ones in the assembly can help to resolve the quarrels in a right and Biblical manner by praying with and for them and by comforting them. Besides such matters as these, those in responsibility can arrange for certain brethren to come to the assistance of the poor who may be facing great difficulty in surviving physically.

Moreover, if there are accidents which occur among the brothers and sisters, those responsible leaders in the assembly can send those maturer brothers or sisters to make whatever needful special arrangement is required. In case you responsible ones hear such news, you should notify those brothers or sisters to go and help. Send money to the poor, give food to the hungry, and supply clothes to the naked. Comfort those who need comfort. Visit those in prison, pray for the sick (cf. Matthew 25:35-36). Help to solve every kind of family problem.

A Foolish Thought

I do not know when the following foolish thought came into existence. Many people seem to have the foolish notion that the church does not have any problems. Let us recall, however, that there were problems from the moment the church began. Do not ever think that if there are problems, this means that the church is wrong. Please recall that not many days after Pentecost the church experienced the incident of Ananias and Sapphira (Acts 5:1-11). And not many days later, there was the exposure of the lack of supply for the Hellenistic widows (Acts 6:1-6). And not long after that there arose the martyrdom of Stephen (Acts 6:7-7:60). Then later Peter was imprisoned (Acts

12:1-17). Such problems, difficulties, and adverse circumstances happened all the time in the Early Church. From ancient times till now the church has always had problems and challenges of various kinds. A true church is continually encountering problems. I do not know where or how such a foolish notion originated. No church is ever free from difficulty. She always experiences blessings on the one hand and numerous problems on the other.

Most of the local churches at the time of the apostles had problems. Among the seven local churches cited in the book of Revelation (chs. 2-3), five were faulty and thus had problems. Moreover, one of them had no blame leveled against her by the Lord, which was the church in Smyrna; even so, she had to endure much suffering that resulted in martyrdom for some of her members. And though one church among these seven—that at Philadelphia—was praised by the Lord for there being nothing wrong or unpraiseworthy in her life, nevertheless, we can infer from the Lord's further word of commendation, "Thou hast kept the word of my patience," that the Philadelphia church in fact encountered many difficulties which required much patience on the part of the believers there in order for the church to overcome. They were able to keep and maintain the word of the Lord's patience, having passed through what we would term adverse or uninviting circumstances of every kind. So let us never claim that if a church has no difficulty and passes through life peacefully, that that is the one and only necessary proof that she has been blessed by the Lord. On the contrary, it cannot be asserted that if a church has many problems, that proves that she is not blessed by the Lord.

Fifth—Taking Care of Brethren
Who Either Go Out or Come In

Writing Commendatory Letter Is Not Final Responsibility

On behalf of a brother or sister who goes forth elsewhere, writing a commendatory letter is not the last duty. I hope there would be three to five or even eight to ten brothers and/or sisters who would undertake two relevant tasks. First, someone or ones would be responsible to correspond with that traveling brother or sister. They should write once a week or at least twice a month to inform him or her concerning the condition of the church meetings at home or of the situation of the brothers and sisters who remain behind in the home church. We must not be careless in undertaking such a task. This, too, is a work of service.

Write to the Church Where That One Goes

And second, I continually have the thought that for brethren who go out, writing commendatory letters is not the last work of service. After a month or so has passed, someone should write to the church where that saint has gone, asking the brethren there concerning the spiritual welfare of the brother or sister who has come into their midst. Expect them to reply as to how they are helping him or her. I would here observe that a large church with many members may end up not giving answer to your inquiry. For it often happens that the people in a large assembly can turn out to be lazy, since even a church as a whole can be lazy. On the other hand, let me also observe that if a local church undertakes to take on and carry many burdens, such an assembly cannot be lazy—no matter how large or small she is. Brethren there must and will reply. They may tell you that they have taken care of that brother or sister or else report that they have not cared for that one. You may then write in response and suggest that later on they should pay more attention to that visitor or visitors.

For Those Who Arrive

I would also hope that the brothers and sisters will be faithful to serve those who arrive from outside. This, too, is a priority function. The time expended on behalf of such a one need not be lengthy. For after two or three months have elapsed, such brethren from outside shall themselves become local members of the church. Thus, those who had taken care of them may now take care of other new arrivals.

Our Way Today Must Be Service by the Entire Church

Our way of serving today will be drastically different from before. Do not think that you are all right because you have done many works of service and are experienced. Today we will totally change. Our new way is going to be different from the Protestants as well as the Catholics. Ours shall be the proper way of the whole church serving, as called for in the New Testament.

I hope the brethren here will pay special attention to this matter. If any of you go elsewhere to work, you may easily forget the vision we have discussed at some length today. Hopefully, each time you go out to work you will have this vision ever before you. You can work with vision; you cannot work without vision (cf. Proverbs 29:18). Perhaps what you are doing today is according to what you have seen before. Though you are still burdened, it may seem useless because brothers and sisters as a whole have not come forth and done works of service. Nevertheless, let us not be governed by how difficult is the way or how many will criticize this new way. The issue before us all is whether or not we have seen this way of service and are willing to implement it. If we are clear on this issue, let us apply all our strength and energy to it by causing all in the church to work. Whether there are many or few who have grasped hold of this vision, the church must follow this way.

Let me declare that if there are two thousand brothers and sisters in a local church but only five hundred are serving while the other fifteen hundred are not, then that will be a most surprising outcome. But should there be in a local church only five hundred brothers and sisters, and all five hundred are serving, then that will be extremely good and right. Otherwise, the weight of the burden is beyond the carrying by a far lesser number who end up doing all the works of service in that church.

Chapter Six

Gifts, Ministries and Functions

And the twelve, having called the multitude of the disciples to them, said, It is not right that we, leaving the word of God, should serve tables. Look out therefore, brethren, from among yourselves seven men, well reported of, full of the Holy Spirit and wisdom, whom we will establish over this business: but we will give ourselves up to prayer and the ministry of the word.

Acts 6:2-4

Gifts, Functions and Ministries

"Now there are diversities of gifts, but the same Spirit. And there are diversities of ministrations, and the same Lord. And there are diversities of workings, but the same God, who worketh all things in all" (I Corinthians 12:4-6). Three things are mentioned here: gifts, ministries, and functions or workings. Gifts belong to the Holy Spirit, functions belong to God, and ministries, to the Lord. These three come from the triune God. Formerly, many emphasized gifts only, they did not pay attention to ministries and functions. We realize that unless we know the place of ministry and function, we will not be able to know the value of gift. Gift is given to produce ministry, and ministry is given to produce function.

Gift can be taken to signify a person's ability, ministry can be understood as being a person's work, and function can be taken to mean the result of a person's work. For example, in the construction industry there are plasterers, masons and carpenters. They have different abilities. Some are good at laying down floors, some are good at creating windows, whereas others are good at building doors. These various abilities can be compared to the diversity gifts mentioned in the above-quoted Bible passage in I Corinthians 12 and elsewhere in Scripture. Each and every member of God's church has a certain gift. And all these gifts are given by the Holy Spirit. Even so, though all such gifts are different, the Holy Spirit is one. Each believer has a different gift, but all must be under the control of the Holy Spirit (see vv. 4, 11).

The Holy Spirit gives each member in the body of Christ his or her gift, thus allowing each such person to do something in contributing to the upbuilding of the body of Christ. The Holy Spirit grants a given gift according to plan. And we all have been given these gifts in order to do work according to the arrangement of the Lord. Whatever works are from the Lord are our ministries. It is not unlike a builder who constructs houses in various places, and many workers will be sent forth to those many places. Some of them are specialists who can lay down floors, and so they are sent forth to lay down the floors. On the other hand, some other workers are specialists who are able to make the doors, and hence, they will be sent out to create doors. Thus, it can be said that those who are sent forth have special abilities: possessing varying gifts, they are sent forth to perform their special works: their abilities are their gifts, and their works are their ministries. And the end result is that all arrive at the purpose of the Lord.

This can be illustrated by seeing the difference between the work of Paul and that of Apollos. We are told in Scripture that whereas Paul planted, Apollos watered, and God has given the increase of their labors (I Corinthians 3:6). And thus, God's increase is the effect. Both Paul and Apollos each had a distinctive ability; and then the Lord sent them out to work according to each's ability. Due to the difference between each of their abilities, they were sent out to accomplish different ministries.

We can therefore conclude from this illustration that a person's handiwork is that person's gift. And thus, each person is able to do what the manager wants each to do, and that becomes each person's ministry. And the result of each person's different ministry constitutes that person's usefulness. Today we all need to ask ourselves individually before the Lord, What is the gift that You have given me?—What, after all, is my ministry? For God has launched a great movement throughout the universe. Yet how will He accomplish the goal of this movement? It shall always be through the Holy Spirit. He gives gifts, and God will coordinate all these various gifts in order to arrive at His purpose. Our responsibilities are simply to exercise our gifts faithfully and work according to the ministries which the Lord has appointed to each. We do not need to be concerned about the effect—"the increase"—for that is the Lord's business.

I Corinthians 12 identifies gifts as coming from the Holy Spirit, services as coming from the Lord, and workings or functions or operations, as being from God; thus revealing to us the source for each. Paul may plant a seed, and Apollos may water the later plant, but it is God who effects the increase. Paul has the ministry of planting, Apollos has that of watering, but what causes the plant to grow depends entirely on God.

The Classifications of Gifts and Ministries

From the Bible we learn that gifts may be of two kinds, whose workings shall result in two kinds of ministries. But whereas one classification of gifts is for serving God, the other classification is for bearing responsibility in the local assembly. All the gifts and ministries are within these two areas. Those who labor for the Lord are sent out to work, while those who bear responsibilities in the assembly will take care of local affairs. All the brothers and sisters in the local assembly each have one or the other of these two kinds of service. The New Testament book of Acts tells us about these two kinds of service in the local assembly or church. One is spiritual and the other is physical. There is that kind of service which is spiritual in nature; for example, the apostles said that they would devote themselves to prayer and to preaching God's word. And there is the kind of service which is physical in nature; for example, brother Stephen and the other six were to bear responsibility in taking care of food distribution.

Know One's Ministry

In conclusion today, I would like to speak to my fellow workers. Each of you must clearly know your ministry. First, you need to find out whether your ministry is a serving the Lord in your being sent out, or in bearing responsibility in the local assembly. Each of you needs to find out if you are to devote yourselves to pray and preach or to serve the table—to learn whether your service is spiritual or physical in character. Peter said, "We need to devote ourselves to pray and preach," and such was spiritual ministry. But, then, seven deacons were chosen to do the kind of service that was physical in nature.

If you are clear that the Lord calls you to pray and preach, then you need to proceed diligently in that direction. But if you are unsure, then you should remain in the other ministry.

Chapter Seven

The Function of the Anointing Oil

And he poured of the anointing oil on Aaron's head, and anointed him, to hallow him. ... And Moses took of the anointing oil, and of the blood that was on the altar, and sprinkled it on Aaron, on his garments, and on his sons, and on his sons' garments with him; and hallowed Aaron, his garments, and his sons, and his sons' garments with him.

Leviticus 8:12, 30

The Spirit of the Lord is upon me, because he has anointed me to preach glad tidings to the poor; he has sent me to preach to captives deliverance, and to the blind sight, to send forth the crushed delivered, to preach the acceptable year of the Lord.

Luke 4:18-19

Jesus who was of Nazareth: how God anointed him with the Holy Spirit and with power; who went through all quarters doing good, and healing all that were under the power of the devil, because God was with him.

Acts 10:38

And [as to] yourselves, the unction [or, anointing] which ye have received from him abides in you, and ye have not need that any one should teach you; but as the same unction teaches you as to all things, and is true and is not a lie, and even as it has taught you, ye shall abide in him.

I John 2:27

Behold, how good and how pleasant it is for brethren to dwell together in unity! Like the precious oil upon the head, that ran down upon the beard, upon Aaron's beard, that ran down to the hem of his garments; as the dew of Hermon that descendeth on the mountains of Zion; for there hath Jehovah commanded the blessing, life for evermore.

Psalms 133:1-3

Oil before God Is Sanctification

Leviticus chapter 8 speaks of Aaron being anointed, chapter 9 speaks of his sacrifice to God. Before David became Israel's king, he was anointed by Samuel. Thus the anointing upon David occurred before he began his God-given ministry to serve God as king over His people (I Samuel 16:12-13). This clearly indicates to us that ministry comes only after anointing. For a person to undertake his ministry before God, he needs first to be anointed before Him. This principle was true with respect to the Lord Jesus, for did He not declare the following word from Isaiah: "The Spirit of the Lord is upon me, because he has anointed me to preach glad tidings to the poor, he has called me to preach to captives deliverance, and to the blind sight, to send forth the crushed delivered, to preach the acceptable year of the Lord." Hence, we learn from God's word that for a person to be usable in God's hand, he must first be anointed before Him. If a person has not been anointed before God, he can neither serve nor work.

Be advised, however, that this matter of being anointed can easily turn into a mere formality. To better understand this statement, perhaps some background is needed. Is it not true that, Biblically speaking, we easily join oil and power together? Indeed, oil—the symbol in Scripture of the Spirit—and power do go together. For as we earlier read from Acts 10, God had anointed Jesus of Nazareth with both the Holy Spirit and power. Therefore, based on God's word, the Holy Spirit and power are in fact joined together: the Holy Spirit is the very power of God. Furthermore, the Holy Spirit becoming power in man is a direct result of that man being anointed with oil.

Nevertheless, it needs to be realized that the Holy Spirit becoming power to or in a man is never God's primary thought—which is to say, that a person being anointed is not, in the first instance, for the sake of—say—speaking in tongues nor for performing miracles. Rather, the primary meaning and purpose for a person to receive anointing is for that one to be separated to God.

It is important for us to recognize that though there are many places in the Old Testament where the anointing has been mentioned, nevertheless, we do not notice anointing and power being connected. And this is because in the Old Testament there is but one thought being presented when anointing is being mentioned, which is, to show that the person or persons who are being anointed belong to God. If, to use a human example, we put our seal on a letter or document, we are saying that the latter belongs to us. God anoints with oil in order to show that this or that person belongs to Him. Thus we see from the Old Testament that anointing is for sanctification—indicating that that person has been set apart for God.

We can conclude, then, that the first condition for ministry is for the minister to be wholly for God. No one can have any ministry before God if that one has not first been separated to Him. Only the person who has been sanctified to God will have any ministry by which to serve Him. Only those sanctified to

Jehovah can have any works of ministry. If the condition or state of sanctification undergoes a change, the ministry of the person shall also undergo a change. When the Holy Spirit came upon the Lord Jesus at His baptism, the first result to be noticed was not His commencing to minister but was God declaring from heaven, "This is my beloved Son" (Matthew 3:17). Hence, in the first instance, anointing is an indication of God's possession: that here was a Man about whom God could say that He belonged to Him. Only *then* could God send Jesus forth and use Him in demonstration of power. And as a result, the gospel was preached to the poor, the blind were able to see, the crushed were delivered, and the acceptable year of the Lord could be preached.

Anointing Is Power to Others

We are told that God anointed Jesus of Nazareth with the Holy Spirit and with power; and that He then traveled everywhere doing good works and healing all those who were oppressed by demons. All this that the Lord Jesus did in works of service was the result of God having anointed Him. What, then, is the ointment with which Jesus was anointed? It was the Holy Spirit and His power. If we can see and understand this, it is something truly wonderful and precious: the ointment in us is the Holy Spirit and in others it is the power: in us is the Holy Spirit as ointment, whereas His power is manifested in others. Therefore, if we have the Holy Spirit's anointing, people in contact with us will experience His power in themselves.

Hence, if we are sanctified and separated to God, we will just naturally exert His power upon and in others. If we are consecrated before God, there will automatically be manifested His power in others. Power is therefore not the first consideration but the second one. If the matter of our being separated to God has been favorably resolved, then the question of His power in others will have quite naturally been resolved favorably as well. But whenever consecration or separation becomes a problem, the power and the working of His power also become a problem. If, though, sanctification is present, the anointing of the Holy Spirit will quite naturally be powerful. We can see this clearly in the lives of David and Aaron and the Lord Jesus.

Anointing Is a Lesson for Us to Learn

As we learn to serve God, we readily discover a spiritual fact. For instance, when you stand up to speak, if you speak for God, you have the anointing upon you; indeed, you sense you are not speaking by or from yourself but rather, you realize that the Spirit's anointing is with you. Your words may be ordinary and simple, yet the more you speak, the more powerful you have become because you sense the anointing upon you. And as you sense the anointing upon you, the audience commences sensing the power. On the other hand, there may be times when as you are speaking, you feel as though you are like a tire that is leaking air: you do not sense any anointing and others present do not sense any power. The explanation for the difference is here: having the anointing of the Spirit is having power, having no such anointing means having no power; if, though, there be the anointing, you shall experience soothing ointment, and power shall be manifested in others.

"And [as to] yourselves, the unction [or, anointing] which ye have received from him abides in you, and ye have not need that any one should teach you; but as the same unction teaches you as to all things, and is true and is not a lie, and even as it has taught you, ye shall abide in him" (I John 2:27). These words include much, for we are told here that the Spirit's anointing teaches a person regarding all things. The teaching of the anointing is totally different from man's teaching. The teaching of the anointing does not necessarily tell a person the *content* of many things nor do so with many words. Rather, this verse informs us that the anointing tells us *about* or *concerning* all those many things. Nevertheless, it all depends on whether the anointing is present: it is something quite special.

Let us say, for example, that there is something which the Lord may or may not wish you to do. If He does in fact wish you to do it, and if the anointing is present, then if you begin to accomplish the matter, you will serve with the anointing, and thus you will know that this is right for you to do. On the other hand, if you should disobey the anointing by not doing the thing in question, your sense at that moment can be likened to a leaking tire tube of air; and thus you will know that it was wrong for you not to have done the thing which the Lord had wished you to accomplish.

The nature of the teaching of the anointing is neither doctrine nor reason. If it is either doctrine or reason, then our brain must undergo a change, for the reasoning of our mind is far distant from that of the mind of God. We are unable to understand God's reasoning. Hence, our yes or no is dependent upon the presence or absence of the anointing. The movement of the latter does not depend on whether or not it is reasonable or logical.

Therefore, our yes-or-no action-responses depend on the presence or absence of the anointing. They do not express themselves according to whether they are in line with reason or logic. In this matter of the anointing, then, all the children of God need to learn a lesson, which is, that in following God let us not be guided by reason; instead, let us be guided by the Holy Spirit who will grant us an anointed sensing. Many times we want to take a certain action which seems reasonable to us, but when we begin to move forward, we feel we are alone, for the Lord is not present. This indicates that you are wrong.

Suppose you are talking with people. If there is no anointing, the more you speak, the less power you sense, you feel like a tire tube which has run out of air. On the other hand, if you sense a burden of the Lord within, the more you speak, the more you will sense a divine amen within. The Lord's burden begins to lighten, and thus you know that this is His doing. For this reason, if you do not sense the anointing within, you are finished if you begin to move forward. Whenever you are without anointing, the more you work, the colder within, and others cannot sense any power coming forth from you. Only when you are being anointed of the Holy Spirit will others feel divine power coming out from you. In such a situation the anointing within is teaching or knowledge in you but it manifests power in others.

Many brothers and sisters seek after power just as many are seeking after life. Yet the word of God says to us that death works in us but life works in others (II Corinthians 4:12). Whoever seeks for life in himself fails to gain life. It is only when death works in us who are God's children that life works in others. Similarly let us not seek for ourselves to have only the anointing. There must also be present the after effect of the anointing, which is the Holy Spirit's power coming forth. For when the anointing is in us, divine power must come forth in others. By the same token, were we to seek only for power, the power probably will not be manifested.

Sadly, some children of God seek for a power that can be felt, that which they themselves could feel and trust in. But this is totally wrong. What we as God's servants need to pay attention to is not power but anointing. Do we abide in Christ through the teaching of the anointing? For what is not done according to the teaching of the anointing will not have spiritual reality in life. It is when the anointing is there that people will find help. They shall touch life, even the Lord himself.

There is another facet to be noticed in this matter of the anointing. Anointing is not to be experienced by one believer only, it is for the entire body of Christ. The ointment that was poured on Aaron's head flowed to his beard and then down upon his entire skirt. As was intimated by the psalmist of old, it is only under such a total anointing that one can witness the good and pleasant character of it. We therefore do not seek for the teaching of the anointing in our individual selves alone, we seek for the Lord's teaching of the anointing in the entire many-membered body of Christ. We not only seek for the teaching of the anointing within each one of us, we also look for the sensing of the anointing in the whole body of Christ.

I will illustrate this facet by means of relating the following true incident. One day there was a brother who was expected to lead a local church meeting but who felt emptiness within; so he asked another brother to go and lead that meeting instead. While this other brother was on his way, he felt he should give his testimony. Though he usually did not like to give his testimony, on *this* occasion he felt the anointing within him to do so and obeyed the inner anointing. It so happened that two friends, who were invited to the meeting and who had been there before but could not understand the preaching, had remained absent for some time thereafter. This particular evening, however, they were persuaded by a friend of theirs to attend the church meeting. Moreover, present this same evening were some brothers who were praying for them that they might hear the right word. As a result, the testimony of the reluctant but obedient speaker turned out to be especially for these two friends in particular.

This is but one example of what it means to be led by the inner anointing. Let us bear in mind, however, that we are not able to serve beyond the leading of the anointing within us. To whatever extent is the anointing, just so should be the extent of our serving God in a given situation. We must keep within the bounds of what the Lord has revealed to us by means of the inner anointing of the Holy Spirit.

It is when we truly sense the anointing that we begin to understand what the ministry of the Lord is. This is because only when we have the anointing in us do we actually have His word. So we serve God through the inner anointing, for it is He who calls our attention to His instruction. It is God who gives us the word with which to serve His children and the unbelievers.

Finally, I hope brothers and sisters will do all their service based on sanctification. The anointing which God grants to you proves that you are His—that you belong to Him. With the anointing, you have a sense that you are the Lord's. With the anointing you also sense that the Lord is calling you to serve. And as you sense all this in accordance with the anointing, these sensings will become power transferred to, and manifested in, others. Such power is not the result of any dead voice from a preaching platform, nor is it either miracle or wonder. No, it is as you are serving under the inner anointing that God will enable others to touch life. For such power is none other than the anointing of His Spirit.

May God bless us that we may abide in the Lord according to the teaching of the anointing.

Chapter Eight

Gifts and Ministries

And he has given some apostles, and some prophets, and some evangelists, and some shepherds and teachers, for the perfecting of the saints; with a view to the work of the ministry, with a view to the edifying of the body of Christ.

Ephesians 4:11-12

This Ephesians passage mentions four or five kinds of gifts; namely, apostles, prophets, evangelists, shepherds and teachers. The purpose of these five gifted ministries is to edify the saints in order that each member of Christ's body will fulfill his or her own ministry. The ministries of the saints are of many kinds, but these five ministries given to the church are special: they are to help the saints to fulfill *their* ministries. So these five special ministries minister to all the saints in a local church. In other words, those who have been gifted with these special ministries are ministers to the other saints in the church in fulfilling their individual ministries. This kind of relationship can be likened to that which exists between certain banks and the other banks. Each and every bank has its own business, and these special banks are to help manage the businesses which have been handed over to them by their banks. It can also be said that the relationship between the aforementioned five special ministers and the ordinary saints in fulfilling their ministries can be likened as well to the teachers in teacher training schools or colleges who educate others who seek to become teachers themselves; and hence, they are teachers of potential teachers.

Since the works of these five special ministries are for the purpose of perfecting the saints in general towards the fulfillment of their own ministries, they should at least have one or more of these five kinds of gifts, without which they are unable to fulfill their ministries to the saints. An ordinary believer may not have God's calling to become one of these five kinds of special ministers; nevertheless, according to nature, the work he or she will have produced stands on the same level as that of a specially-called minister.

Matthew 25 tells us that the Lord distributes talents to His servants: some receive five, some receive two, and some, one. Every one of His servants has at least one talent. According to the distribution of these talents, they are either ordinary or special in character. Those with one talent receive one ordinary gift, and those with five or two talents receive five or two special gifts—as the case may be. The words prophecy and teaches mentioned in Romans 12:6-7 reflect the gifts to the church of prophets and teachers. And hence, the gift to the church of apostles mentioned in Ephesians 4:11 may not necessarily be an indication that those apostles had seen and were each a witness to the resurrection of the Lord—one of the necessary qualifications for being one of the twelve apostles of Christ (Acts 1:15-26).

Joints of Supply

Other than the five specially-gifted ministers cited in Ephesians 4, all the other saints in the church, in the exercise of their talents or gifts, must submit to these five specially-gifted ministers. This will keep any of the saints from becoming proud of his/her gift. And the word until stated in Ephesians 4:13 indicates that these five specially-gifted ministers and their ministries will continue on till all the saints throughout the entire body of Christ arrive at the unity of the faith and of the knowledge of the Son of God, till all arrive at the full-grown man, and till all arrive at the measure of the stature of the fullness of Christ. Thus today there are still apostles, prophets, etc., etc. The explanation set forth in Ephesians 4:13-16 further proves that these five kinds of gifted ministers and their ministries are still available to the church "according to the working in its measure of each one part" (v. 16b); and the "each one part" here has reference to the "joint of supply" of verse 16a.

Human biology can perhaps be helpful here in better understanding what the apostle Paul is saying in these latter verses. We may say that human body organs are of two kinds: one kind can be designated as spending organs, such as the hands and feet that by their various movements expend energy and strength; whereas the other kind can be called supply organs, such as the mouth, ears and eyes which receive the necessaries of life from the outside. And so it can be said that the five special kinds of ministers and their ministries can be likened to supply organs. As you and I are before the Lord, we need to ask to be organs of supply to the rest of the saints in the body of Christ: saints receive supply and we also can experience the joy of being channels of supply to others. If you do not have this special kind of gift in ministry, then let those who do have such gift serve as organs of supply to the church.

Know Your Ministry

The passage in I Corinthians 12:28-30 mentions nine gifts—with those of apostles, prophets, and teachers leading the list. These three leading gifts are also mentioned in Ephesians 4. One might therefore conclude that these three are especially viewed as primary gifts while the other six can be characterized as miraculous in nature and of secondary importance. Due to their continued presence and availability, the church can be built.

We must now ask ourselves: Who among us have these five gifts? This we need to determine before God. If you are among those who have these special gifts, then you will need to discern what is your particular ministry, because your particular ministry is closely related to those of others. If, however, you are not clear concerning your ministry, and yet you go forward without clearly knowing, then you will be as though kicking against others' legs; for as you advance you, as it were, will be stepping on others' toes. Consequently, we shall discover that the ministry of a worker has its limits. We each can only work within the bounds of our particular ministry. Only according to the boundary limits of our individual ministries can we serve. Only on special occasions may we work outside the boundary of our particular ministry.

There is a relationship between one's personal ministry and that of others. One kind of ministry may require us to lead, whereas other kinds of ministry may require us to follow. We should therefore be clear as to our limits, and thus work accordingly. Otherwise, we will be in conflict with the ministry of other servants of God. Those who are not sure of their particular ministry should be careful to wait patiently before God. Let us not undertake our individual ministry carelessly. The conflict which may occur among workers is largely that which concerns gifts, it therefore concerns ministries. For instance, suppose a person in the construction industry is a plasterer who nonetheless wants to do the work of a carpenter, a work of another which he is not able to do. Let us clearly realize that all ministries are appointed by the Lord and all gifts are given by the Holy Spirit. The coordination between the workers and the local church should be an harmonious one, with neither the workers nor the church being troublesome. The aim of the local church is to enable the work to grow. Hence, the responsible brothers should not resist the work of the ministry nor hinder the work of the workers.

Apostolic Ministry and Local Church Ministry

The Bible separates the works of the workers from the church. The burden for the workers' works are upon the shoulders of the apostles, whereas the burden of the local church is on the shoulders of the elders or responsible brothers. In their work apostles are for all the churches, while elders in their work are only for one local church. In the case of Peter, he was an apostle as well as an elder. His service as an apostle was for all the churches; at the same time, his service as an elder in the church at Jerusalem was only for that local church. On the one hand he served the local church as an elder, and on the other hand he served also all the churches as an apostle. Whether it be a local ministry or the ministry of a worker abroad, they are all ministries. That English word worker is derived from the original Greek term *diakoneo*—which is the Greek source for the English word deacon. At the time of the Early Church, whenever a locality began to be supplied with ministry, there was no single person who was responsible. The result was that a few people would temporarily take up all kinds of responsibilities. But when the number of saints increased, more responsible ones would be manifested, with the temporary ones able to draw back, thus allowing the manifested ones to take charge. A responsible brother should not only be gifted but also be irreproachable, have a good testimony with outsiders, be hospitable, a lover of good, sober-minded, just, holy, and self-controlled (I Timothy 3:1-7, Titus 1:5-9).

Apostolic Authority and Local Church Authority

The New Testament reveals to us that different people had different ministries. Apollos had his ministry, Silas had his; but so did Timothy, Epaphras, Titus, Mark, Luke, etc. have their different ministries. Some among them were under Paul's management while some others were not. This position of management must be mutually agreed upon. We must not use the way of today's Christianity in which authority stands above ministers. The notion of organization in Christianity calls for the direction of the minister, and so the latter must act and do accordingly. But God's way is not so. He desires the gifted to mutually obey.

True authority comes from deep dealings of the cross in a person. He who directs others must himself be able to be submitted to others. Even the experience of Paul was no exception to this principle. He could send out Timothy, Titus and others, but he himself also recognized and received the charge of the brethren in whose midst he found himself (e.g., see Acts 21:17-26). If there be a problem along this line between or among believers, and a brother or sister cannot obey, the first question to be asked is, Has that person had a prior problem in his/her communion with God? Whether a believer agrees or not, that one must obey if such is required.

Obey Authority

Some saints entertain the notion that to have been delivered out of the denominational system is to have been freed from all authority. Their thinking is that being delivered out of denominationalism has delivered them from all human authority. Not so, for we who are no longer within the framework of denominationalism are still under the authority of God; and in our lives and in our works He has established many representative authorities in order that we may learn obedience. If any believer should say that he/she cannot find an earthly authority to obey, that one must surely have a problem. For let us consider for a few moments the extended family as an example. In the extended family we can readily discern that there are various authorities present: the parents are the authority over the children, the grandparents are the authority over the parents, elder brothers and sisters are the authority over the younger siblings. Whenever you are at home, you are obligated to obey authority. Then, too, whenever you go outside, the policeman on the road is likewise your authority and you must obey him. In our lives we should never disobey legitimate authority simply because we do not feel like obeying.

If a responsible brother wishes to be clear as to whether or not he should be one, the best way for him to find out is for him to ask the brothers and sisters in the church what they think about this. He should ask them if he should continue to be one. In responding, those brothers and sisters should not hesitate to be candid: if, in their estimation, that responsible brother has been conducting himself well, he may continue; but if not, he should resign.

Authoritative Prayer[*]

If in a church meeting there should arise a problem beyond human dealing, then the church should pray an authoritative prayer, asking the Lord to effect the necessary discipline in the situation. If the work of that local church is truly the Lord's, then the Lord's throne will back up the church's prayer. In such times the responsible brothers must exercise the Lord's power to deal with untoward cases.

We need to help people to see that the church today is the place where the Lord's power and throne are. All who are in the church should recognize the authority in the church. The workers are the Lord's representatives; and hence, the Lord's authority is in them. I Timothy 5:17, I Thessalonians 5:12-13a, and Hebrews 13:7, 17 declare that a worker should be shown and/or receive high regard, double honor, and obedience. Such words in Scripture need to be read often to the church brethren so that they know there is authority in the church. They need to respect and obey authority.

---

[*] For a detailed explication of this subject, consult Watchman Nee, *The Prayer Ministry of the Church* (New York: Christian Fellowship Publishers, 1973, ch. 4).—*Publishers*

Chapter Nine

<u>Sin against Ministry</u>

And when they came to Nachon's threshing-floor, Uzzah reached after the ark of God, and took hold of it; for the oxen had stumbled. And the anger of Jehovah was kindled against Uzzah; and God smote him there for his error; and there he died by the ark of God. ... And David was afraid of Jehovah that day, and said, How shall the ark of Jehovah come to me?

II Samuel 6:6-7, 9

And they withstood Uzziah the king, and said to him, It is not for thee, Uzziah, to burn incense to Jehovah, but for the priests the sons of Aaron, that are consecrated to burn incense. Go out of the sanctuary; for thou hast transgressed; neither shall it be for thine honour from Jehovah Elohim. And Uzziah was wroth; and he had a censer in his hand to burn incense; and while he was wroth with the priests, the leprosy rose up in his forehead before the priests in the house of Jehovah, beside the incense altar. And Azariah the chief priest and all the priests looked upon him, and behold, he was leprous in his forehead, and they thrust him out from thence; even he himself hasted to go out, because Jehovah had smitten him.

II Chronicles 26:18-20

And Jehovah said to Aaron, Thou and thy sons and thy father's house with thee shall bear the iniquity of the sanctuary; and thou and thy sons with thee shall bear the iniquity of your priesthood. And thy brethren also, the tribe of Levi, the tribe of thy father, bring near with thee, that they may unite with thee, and minister unto thee; but thou and thy sons with thee shall serve before the tent of the testimony. And they shall keep thy charge, and the charge of the whole tent: only they shall not come near to the vessels of the sanctuary and to the altar, that they may not die, and you as well as they. And they shall unite with thee, and keep the charge of the tent of meeting, for all the service of the tent; and no stranger shall come near to you. And ye shall keep the charge of the sanctuary, and the charge of the altar; that there come no wrath any more upon the children of Israel. ... But thou and thy sons with thee shall attend to your priesthood for all that concerneth the altar, and for that which is inside the veil; and ye shall perform the service: I give you your priesthood as a service of gift, and the stranger that cometh near shall be put to death. And Jehovah spoke to Aaron, And I, behold, I have given thee the charge of my heave-offerings, of all the hallowed things of the children of Israel; to thee have I given them, because of the anointing, and to thy sons by an everlasting statute.

Numbers 18:1-5, 7-8

Those people in Old Testament times who were charged with performing the ministry of priesthood served God with glory. Such ministry was the foundation of all the other ministries, for without this ministry all other ministries became vain and useless. Those other ministries could not please God nor be accepted by Him. Furthermore, we discover that in the age of the New Testament—which includes our present day—the ministry of the prophets is the leading ministry. Nevertheless, even this ministry—that of the prophets—must be based, and *is* based, on priestly ministry, too. Otherwise, it can only be recognized and accounted as external and empty: it will only be ministry undertaken towards men and not towards God. We need to realize that spiritual service is of two kinds: one is a working *for* God, whereas the other is a serving of God himself. Please therefore understand and keep in mind that only this second kind of service is pleasing to God.

Sin against the Sanctuary

From chapter 18 of the book of Numbers we learn that God told Aaron, saying (1) that he, his sons and his kinsmen shall bear the sin against the sanctuary; (2) that God said to the Levites that they should keep their charge and guard the sanctuary, but that they should not come near to the vessels of the sanctuary nor to the altar; and (3) that no one else was to come near to them. Elsewhere in Old Testament Scripture we learn that God had clearly indicated what were the various sins which people might commit against Him but which would not result in death. However, from this same chapter 18 of Numbers we learn that there is one particular sin which results in death: the sin against the sanctuary—which is to say, the sin against the holy ministry. A person committing such sin had no chance of being forgiven nor of escaping death.

Now what exactly was this sin against the sanctuary? Before it can be defined it will probably be necessary for us to refresh ourselves as to what exactly ministry is. We have previously come to understand that all ministries come out of, or must go through the experience of, death and resurrection. Let us recall how Aaron's rod had to be placed before God and, as it were, had to experience life out of death. That rod of Aaron's had no life in itself, for it was a dead object. Typologically speaking, we need to realize that we who may be called of God to minister are like this rod, dead and useless to Him: nothing with which to offer up and an inability to supply His word, and thus being of absolutely no value to God for His use. Yet recall further that God brought this dry useless rod of Aaron's through death into life, for it began to bud. Its having been placed before God therefore allowed the life of God to flow into it.

Speaking further here and using New Testament terms, we may say, as did the apostle Paul when writing of ministry to God in his Second Corinthians letter, that God has placed a treasure in earthen vessels like Paul for ministry, which treasure is the life that has gone through death and been resurrected (4:1a, 7, 10-12). Speaking still further from the New Testament, we may also say that the experience of Philippians 3:10—which concerns the Lord Jesus' death-and-resurrection experience—has been given to us, but how do we who have been called into the ministry of sharing God's word respond? For instance, looking at this matter negatively, suppose a person attempts to use his cleverness to serve God; it will become evident that such service does not originate from life nor manifest life in himself nor in others. On the contrary, it can only bring in death because that person had not experienced the death to himself and his cleverness that is called for in this Philippians passage.

So what, in New Testament language, is the sin against the sanctuary? It is to serve the Lord without His resurrection life. Many are using their natural zeal to serve God, and such is the sin against the sanctuary. Many of God's servants serve Him with their strong will. Such is also a sinning against the sanctuary. Furthermore, some people who have very clear, bright minds use their clear thinking to manage their personal affairs rather than being guided by the mind of Christ (Philippians 2:5). These same people love to live among the circle of those who are highly spiritual and love to listen to spiritual sermons. Even so, they are as those who listen outside the window, the content of such sermons never becoming the character or conduct of their lives. They in their attitude and behavior have never been touched by any revelation. Their natural strength and individualism have never gone through death. They thus serve God with their natural strength, and that and their continued individualistic nature are an offense to God. This also can be defined as sinning against the sanctuary.

Unless our ministry is accepted by God, it will result in spiritual death. Such service can be likened to what happened to Uzzah upon his stretching out his hand to steady the ark when the oxen carrying the ark of God had stumbled. Uzzah used his unclean hand to steady God's holy object and immediately he was struck down and died. Outwardly speaking, this was a most natural reaction on Uzzah's part, but it went against God's instructions on how to handle the ark. Indeed, Uzzah's action emanated from man's natural strength and fleshly way. It was a serving God contrary to His will and way.

Oftentimes we use our flesh to do the things of God: we speak before God's time, we not having waited for His timing and way: we tend to do things *for* God instead of serving Him himself, and the result is death. Like Uzzah, who experienced physical death as a warning to others, we are stricken with death in our spirits. Let us be reminded of what happened to King Uzziah, who out of his own will sought to do what only the priest was authorized to do in burning incense before God. God immediately afflicted him with leprosy, and finally he died.

In like manner, many people today like to do work in God's temple—the church—they doing what God has not appointed them to do. They have a strong desire to serve, they wishing to do Christian works of various kinds. They deem it to be for them a service of great enjoyment. In so doing, they gradually take charge of all kinds of activities, even to the point of sacrificing themselves in bearing hardships detrimental to their health and well-being. How, someone may ask, can that be wrong? Yet God says that such conduct is the committing of the sin against the sanctuary, and is thus not what He wants, for He has not called them to engage in those activities. Such so-called works of service arise either from sheer human ability or from that which has not passed through the death of the cross unto resurrection life. Such action only brings forth what belongs to the old creation: such things as untransformed eloquence, cleverness, goodness, natural strength, and so forth. They all, if indulged in, become sins against the sanctuary.

Out of God and for God

We can only use what is of God to serve Him. Only by God's ability may we serve the Lord. You may conduct a very enthusiastic meeting, wherein many emotions are being stirred. But if not of God, it is all natural. One day this will be proven to have been a work of wood, grass and straw and thus will not be able to go through fire (I Corinthians 3:12-13). We may even praise God for past blessings, but if such blessings were not produced through death and resurrection, then one day all such so-called blessings will vanish. None will count in the last day.

We all need to be like a dried rod that passes the night before God. It must be a *full* night, not merely ten minutes. We want such a death experience to be over quickly; but God will hide us without using us till it is the following morning. The person who serves God must go through death, and such a person may be a gospel minister or gospel singer. During each such death experience we have no strength to serve and our spiritual wealth is being taken away. Thus, our past joyful knowledge and experience are all surrendered. We may even experience the loss of our prayer life and our testimony may even be buried from sight and sound. Everything may seem to be gloomy and deathly at such times. Yet we are still in God's hands, being placed within the holy place. We refuse to look at ourselves and examine ourselves as to what is of God and what is of self, as to what is natural and what is spiritual. All considerations like these turn into a kind of darkness which we have never experienced before. We can only look off and away to Jesus, fixing our eyes solely upon Him (Hebrews 12:1-2), and believing that resurrection morning shall come. During such a time we must not revert to our own natural devices to speed up the conclusion of this experience. Instead, let God fulfill His perfect work through what some have termed the dark night of the soul.

All works of service must be of the second kind: that of serving God himself. If we are truly intent on serving God, if we serve Him with sincerity, we are truly the priests of God.

Chapter Ten

Added Messages

One—The Relationship between Anointing and Ministry

And he presented the second ram, the ram of consecration; and Aaron and his sons laid their hands on the head of the ram; and one slaughtered it ; and Moses took of its blood, and put it on the tip of Aaron's right ear, and on the thumb of his right hand, and on the great toe of his right foot; and he brought Aaron's sons near, and Moses put of the blood on the tip of their right ear, and on the thumb of their right hand, and on the great toe of their right foot; and Moses sprinkled the blood upon the altar round about. And he took the fat, and the fat tail, and all the fat that was on the inwards, and the net of the liver, and the two kidneys and their fat, and the right shoulder; and out of the basket of unleavened bread that was before Jehovah he took one unleavened cake, and a cake of oiled bread, and one wafer, and put them on the fat and upon the right shoulder; and he gave all into Aaron's hands, and into his sons' hands, and waved them as a wave-offering before Jehovah. And Moses took them from off their hands, and burned them on the altar, over the burnt-offering: they were a consecration-offering for a sweet odour: it was an offering by fire to Jehovah. And Moses took the breast, and waved it as a wave-offering before Jehovah; of the ram of consecration it was Moses' part; as Jehovah had commanded Moses.

And Moses took of the anointing oil, and of the blood that was on the altar, and sprinkled it on Aaron, on his garments, and on his sons, and on his sons' garments with him; and hallowed Aaron, his garments, and his sons, and his sons' garments with him.

Leviticus 8:22-30

And the priest shall take of the blood of the trespass-offering, and the priest shall put it on the tip of the right ear of him that is to be cleansed, and on the thumb of his right hand, and on the great toe of his right foot. And the priest shall take of the log of oil, and pour it into his, the priest's, left hand; and the priest shall dip his right finger in the oil that is in his left hand, and shall sprinkle of the oil with his finger seven times before Jehovah. And of the rest of the oil that is in his hand shall the priest put on the tip of the right ear of him that is to be cleansed, and on the thumb of his right hand, and on the great toe of his right foot, upon the blood of the trespass-offering.

Leviticus 14:14-17

The Spirit of the Lord is upon me, because he has anointed me to preach glad tidings to the poor; he has sent me to preach to captives deliverance, and to the blind sight, to send forth the crushed delivered.

Luke 4:18

Jesus who was of Nazareth: how God anointed him with the Holy Spirit and with power; who went through all quarters doing good, and healing all that were under the power of the devil, because God was with him.

Acts 10:38

And yourselves, the unction [or, anointing] which ye have received from him abides in you, and ye have not need that any one should teach you; but as the same unction teaches you as to all things, and is true and is not a lie, and even as it has taught you, ye shall abide in him.

I John 2:27

Behold, how good and how pleasant it is for brethren to dwell together in unity! Like the precious oil upon the head, that ran down upon the beard, upon Aaron's beard, that ran down to the hem of his garments; as the dew of Hermon that descendeth on the mountains of Zion; for there hath Jehovah commanded the blessing, life for evermore.

Psalms 133:1-3

All ministries only come into being after the Spirit's anointing. Aaron started to fulfill his priestly ministry only after he had received anointing. David also began to fulfill his kingly ministry only after he had been anointed. Elijah likewise started his prophetic ministry only after he was anointed. Even our Lord himself did not commence His public ministry until after the Holy Spirit had descended upon Him at His baptism.

We generally connect anointing and power together. In one sense that is true. Yet, due to our connecting these two, we may neglect or overlook the meaning and significance of the anointing itself. That the Holy Spirit becomes the power of

103

ministry is the result of the anointing; nevertheless, that is not the primary purpose of anointing. Its primary purpose is to sanctify the person or object that is being anointed, that is, for him or it to be separated or consecrated to God. Hence, to be anointed is the first essential of ministry. Only those who have been sanctified to Jehovah God have the privilege of serving the Lord Jesus. Only those whom He had chosen as His disciples could serve Him, and the power surely followed. In any case, the power that accompanies the ministry is not the primary motive for being anointed. Instead, the primary reason is for setting apart a person to and for the Lord. Power will most surely follow, for the Lord cannot but be responsible to supply the enabling power to all those whose ministries He has recognized.

In the life of one whose ministry is to be fulfilled the anointing refers not to power but to the presence of the Holy Spirit: "This is the word of Jehovah…, Not by might, nor by power, but by my Spirit, saith Jehovah of hosts" (Zechariah 4:6). Thus, in the life of any would-be servant of God, the presence of God's Spirit is the sign or indicator of that one having been anointed. To others, however, the sign of his having been anointed might be the presence of influence or power. He who teaches us is the Anointing One, whose teaching is not according to reason but according to His very own Self. In this matter of ministry, we who would be God's ministers must not begin any ministry until He has said, "This man/woman is mine"; only then can that one enter into ministry.

Let us recall that before the Lord Jesus commenced His ministry He himself was anointed at His baptism in the river Jordan, a voice having come out of heaven declaring: "This is my beloved Son" (Matthew 3:16-17). First, God came forth to recognize and to proclaim Jesus as His Son, and only then did Jesus begin His ministry. And no one can deny how very powerful was that ministry of His.

So, it is correct in one sense for us to say that power follows anointing. Instead of anointing being a matter of power, it is really a matter of the holy sovereignty of God. This is to declare that the anointed one has been sanctified by, belongs to, and is under the authority of, God. It is God who acknowledges this person as having been chosen by Him. From God's point of view anointing indicates that He has set apart for himself this or that person; and from man's viewpoint, it signifies a ministry for this or that person to serve Him. God looks not for those who are wise or who possess an enthusiastic nature; rather, He looks for those who bear the marks of the cross on their ears, hands and feet.

We learn from the fourth chapter of Luke's Gospel that before the Lord Jesus had begun to fulfill His ministry He first was baptized in the river Jordan, whose waters therefore spoke of death for Him. Only afterwards did the Holy Spirit—the Anointing One of God—descend upon Jesus. And hence, it can be said that the record of the New Testament here is thus synonymous with the Old Testament narratives concerning both blood and oil. Before any anointing, there must be the shedding of blood on altar and cross. Therefore, no cross experience, no anointing; and if no anointing, no ministry.

Two—Priesthood

We read concerning the cleansing of a leper as well as concerning the consecration of Aaron that blood must be put on their ear, hand and foot; and then oil would be applied to where the blood had been put. We learn from some other Bible passages that blood speaks of redemption and that it is for God. Such passages provide the *objective* view of blood. Here, though, is a Bible passage which provides the *subjective* view, for in the cleansing of a leper and the consecration of Aaron the presence of blood speaks of the subjective work of death in a person. For instance, the placing of blood upon Aaron signified that he had died. By combining the Old Testament narrative with that of the New we come to understand that the placing of sacrificial blood upon ear, hand and foot indicates that a ministering priest of God must allow the cross of Christ to deal with all which God's priest-servant hears, does, and goes about walking. For the anointing oil—representing God's Holy Spirit—cannot be applied upon "un-crucified" flesh but only upon wherever the cross has already done its work.

All this God has explained to us through the apostle Peter's writings:

> Ye also, as living stones, are built up a spiritual house, to be a holy priesthood, to offer up spiritual sacrifices, acceptable to God through Jesus Christ. Because it is contained in scripture, Behold, I lay in Zion a chief corner stone, elect, precious: and he that believeth on him shall not be put to shame. For you therefore that believe is the preciousness: but for such as disbelieve, The stone which the builders rejected, the same was made the head of the corner; and, A stone of stumbling, and a rock of offence; for they stumble at the word, being disobedient: whereunto also they were appointed. But ye are an elect race, a royal priesthood, a holy nation, a people for God's own possession, that ye may show forth the excellencies of him who called you out of darkness into his marvellous light (I Peter 2:5-9 ASV).

We also need to recall the following passage from Exodus:

> They departed from Rephidim, and came into the wilderness of Sinai, and encamped in the wilderness; and Israel encamped there before the mountain. And Moses went up to God and Jehovah called to him out of the mountain, saying, Thus shalt thou say to the

house of Jacob, and tell the children of Israel: Ye have
seen what I have done to the Egyptians, and how I
have borne you on eagles' wings and brought you to
myself. And now, if ye will hearken to my voice indeed
and keep my covenant, then shall ye be my own
possession out of all the peoples—for all the earth is
mine—and ye shall be to me a kingdom of priests, and
a holy nation. These are the words which thou shalt
speak to the children of Israel (Exodus 19:2-6).

We should especially take note of these words from this
same passage: "I have borne you on eagles' wings and brought
you to myself ... and ye shall be to me a kingdom of priests"
(4b, 6a). We realize, then, that the purpose of God in redeeming
His chosen people was to gain for himself a priesthood of
servants. In fact, that was why God had demanded of Pharaoh:
"Let my people go, that they may serve me" (Exodus 8:1b).

God chose Abel, and Abel offered a sacrifice. He also
chose Noah, and Noah built an altar and offered a sacrifice on
it. And then God called to himself a whole race, who became
the Israelite nation of people. After He had redeemed them, He
clearly declared to them the purpose of His redemption. God
wanted them, He said to them through His servant Moses, to be
a "kingdom of priests." Due to their moral and spiritual
declension, however, only a portion of the Israelites became
priests, even though God's *original* purpose was for the entire
race of Israel to be priests. According to the author of the New
Testament book of Hebrews, His thought for Israel was as
follows: "... every high priest taken from amongst men is
established for men in things relating to God, that he may offer
both gifts and sacrifices for sins" (5:1).

From the book of Genesis we learn that God had created
mankind for the sake of fulfilling His will, but the first man He
had created—Adam—failed terribly. God then went forth to
work to recover what was lost in mankind, for we further learn

from Genesis that God first found one man—Abraham; and next, He sought out a family—that of Jacob, whom He later named Israel. In order to train His people for the purpose of accomplishing His original will for mankind, God then brought this family down into Egypt. What He brought to Egypt was a family, but what He ultimately brought out of Egypt was a nation: the Israelites.

Now why should God spend so much energy and time, a period of almost two thousand years, to obtain this nation? He himself told us why. It was ultimately for the purpose of bringing them and us into His very own presence. Yet, the cost in opening up this way was beyond computation, for Jesus— the sacrificial Lamb of God—had to shed His precious blood in opening up this way into God's presence. Therefore, the ministry which we—as the end-time beneficiaries of God's much time, energy and cost expended—undertake today lies within the veil of the most holy place.

Priestly Functions

Each and every child of God is called to be a priest. And each and every priest is appointed to offer up both gifts and sacrifices (Hebrews 5:1, 8:3). How, then, could any child of God ever feel that he/she has nothing to offer up to God? If the priests are to offer up to God "both gifts and sacrifices," it is obviously clear that they do indeed have something to offer up. But in order to have those things with which to offer up to God, they must work for them. Just here, however, lies a problem with many Christians: their work becomes their aim and objective. They merely work for the sake of work.

The New Testament letter to the Hebrews specializes in discussing the subject of priesthood. It reveals in its text the principal aspects relating to priesthood, the overall purpose of which is to draw people to God (see, e.g., 4:16; 6:19; 7:19, 25; 10:19-22). We do not find many commands in this book of Hebrews, but the greatest commandment of those which we do find therein is for His people to come before God. The all-inclusive ministry of the children of God is to come into His presence, and, be it noted, without ever coming *out* from His presence. God brought the children of Israel out of bondage in Egypt (in type, the world) and commanded them to enter into the Promised Land (in type, the Lord himself) which He had spread out before them at the river Jordan crossing. Likewise, He brings *us* out of the world that He might bring us into His abiding presence. So, the overall means by which to accomplish this is the universal priesthood of all His people.

God's ultimate desire is not the obtaining of a kingdom of prophets but a kingdom of priests.

Now unlike as was the case during the Old Testament period, it would appear as though during the New Testament era God's people have respected and honored *prophetic* ministry far more than priestly ministry. Yet God's purpose in His people today is to obtain a priesthood. But what He seeks for is a *universal*, not a limited, priesthood. And hence, what God failed to obtain in and through Israel He will ultimately achieve in and through the church.

In the book of Acts we read this: "... in the assembly which was there [at the city of Antioch], prophets and teachers ... And as they were ministering to the Lord" (13:1-2). These men were prophets and teachers. And as they preached as prophets and taught as teachers, they served the Lord and did their works. However, all these works of service were based on their priesthood. If we first are not priests, we will not be prophets; and therefore, what is important is not whether we have done this or that work, but whether our work has been performed as the work of priests.

Please note, in this regard, that many of the Israelites who came out of Egypt were shepherds. Yet shepherding was not their calling from God, for as we previously learned from Exodus 19, their calling from God was that they were to be for Him a kingdom of priests. Then, too, many of the children of

Israel were craftsmen, yet craftsmanship was not their divine calling, for they also were called by God to be a part of the kingdom of priests to Him. A shepherd might offer up a lamb because he was a shepherd; a craftsman might offer up his handicraft because he was a craftsman; but God would not accept these offerings on such a basis. He could only accept their "gifts and sacrifices" on the ground of priesthood (see again Hebrews 5:1). Hence, the issue for us today is not whether or not we have done a work, but whether or not the work has been done as that of a priest.

In Old Testament times the prophets were honored occasionally. But after God had obtained a people for himself, an altar was no longer something which appeared occasionally; it was henceforth something permanent. It is quite true that Abraham built more than one altar, that Isaac and Jacob each also continued building more altars; but after the children of Israel became a people-unto-God, which became a reality at the time the tabernacle was erected, the altar henceforth stood there forever. Offering was no longer done intermittently; rather, it was done continuously. Moreover, an altar no longer belonged to merely one individual, it now belonged to the corporate body of God's people Israel.

Hence, it can be said that the heart desire of God in building His church is to provide a place for the priesthood to fulfill its functions. Ephesians chapter 2 informs us as follows: "In whom each several building, fitly framed together, growth into a holy temple in the Lord; in whom ye also are built together for a habitation of God in the Spirit" (vv. 21-22 ASV). This becomes true because it is our priesthood which provides the quality to our ministries or else enhances that quality. In the sight of God the value of all our works is calculated on the basis of what percentage of *priestly* function—high to low—has informed those works. The original plan of God for each and every Israelite was for him/her to come to God by means of the altar, for that was, and still is, the essence of priestly function.

Priest and Altar

Now because priestly ministry is the basis of all ministries rendered towards God, therefore, apart from the altar, a priest has no service towards Him. It is the altar which distinguishes Abel from Cain, for Abel had an altar stained with blood. Then, too, in the account of Noah, we see the altar and more. Likewise, in the narrative of Abraham's life, we see the altar again. Wherever we find the chosen ones of God, we find the altar of God.

In the Bible whenever we read about God dealing with His chosen individuals, an altar appeared with sacrifices being offered up to God. The church is called into being to fulfill her priestly ministry, and the content of priestly ministry is to offer up spiritual sacrifices to the Lord. If the church fails here, it fails completely.

Priest and Sacrifice

I Peter 2:5 does not simply say, "built up a spiritual house, to offer spiritual sacrifices"; rather, it reads: "built up a spiritual house, *a holy priesthood*, to offer spiritual sacrifices, acceptable to God by Christ Jesus" (emphasis added). It is only a holy priesthood that can offer up spiritual sacrifices. Hence, the church is not simply that which exists to offer up sacrifices; even more so it is that within which the priesthood is established. My emphasis here concerning the church is not to be placed on how many offerings are going to be offered up but on whether or not a permanent priesthood is going to be established: "In whom ye also are [being] built together for a habitation of God in the Spirit" (Ephesians 2:22). Here is found God's perspective on the matter; whereas man's perspective on the matter is found in I Peter 2:5, for there we see that the spiritual temple is in the process of being built so as to allow the sanctified priesthood therein to offer up spiritual sacrifices.

The book of Hebrews shows us the eternal priesthood, and it is manifested in permanent altar and everlasting sacrifice. The very existence of the church is for the purpose of God's redeemed people to engage in priestly service. Without priestly service there can be no foundation to the church. The unceasing priestly ministry which God is after is expressed in the permanent altar and the everlasting sacrifice. The altar is never vacant of sacrificial offerings; indeed, God insists that the fire which consumes the burnt offerings on the altar is never to be extinguished. The existence of the church is not for the purpose of providing the environment within which God's people can perform works of service—not even for the purpose of providing the corporate environment for them to engage in spiritual warfare together. Far more so, the church's existence is preeminently for the purpose of providing a place on earth within which God's people can express a permanent consecrated life that will satisfy His heart completely.

In other words, the ministry of the church is preeminently the ministry of the priesthood; therefore, all the works of the church are summed up in the act of offering up spiritual sacrifices. This is the all-inclusive service of the church. If we are true priests of God, then the vocation of our entire life is none other than, and nothing less than, to offer up gifts and sacrifices. Note, however, that it is a "*holy* priesthood" which offers up spiritual sacrifices acceptable to God (see again I Peter 2:5). If in offering up sacrifices, God's people are not themselves *sanctified* priests, God's heart will not be satisfied.

The main reason for our being called of God is not to be workers but He clearly calls us to be priests. There are many aspects in works which have the potential of building people up and causing those people to be more interested in the works then otherwise and causing those works to be more satisfying to their flesh. The works of service of the priest, however, are a totally different matter. This is because the ordinary Israelite could easily count how many times he came to offer a sacrifice on the tabernacle/temple altar, but a priest could never compute how many sacrifices he had offered up. For the priest, offering up sacrifices was not something he did randomly or intermittently but something he did *all the time*. In other words, for the Old Testament priest, offering up sacrifices could never be viewed by him as the performing of some isolated acts but as constituting his entire life ministry. He lived for that alone, his whole life being engaged in pretty much nothing but that. Hence, what God expects of His people today is not a Christian life marked by occasional or fragmentary offerings but the establishment of a life of a permanent priest.

Many Christians have written on their calendars the special date of their inaugural consecration; some have even consecrated themselves a number of times over the course of their lives because of having been moved to do so at revival meetings. Yet none of these actions can fully satisfy God's wish and desire towards His people. What He seeks for in His people are not isolated acts of consecration. Instead, what can and will satisfy God's heart is if, as the Christian offers up a sacrifice, the Christian himself ascended to God with it. When each of us goes to bed at night, let us not report to ourselves how many works we have done for God that day but inquire of Him how much of what we have done was truly spiritual sacrifice. How often, at the close of all our days on earth as a Christian, could we have said to the Lord, "O Lord, I place all sacrifices in Thy hands"?

Three—Priestly Ministry

Now there were in Antioch, in the assembly which was there, prophets and teachers ... And as they were ministering to the Lord and fasting, the Holy Spirit said, Separate me now Barnabas and Saul for the work to which I have called them (Acts 13:1a-2).

Upon our having finished a certain work, usually it is followed by a sense of accomplishment which gives the flesh a certain satisfaction. Yet, it is often the case that when sacrificing to God we ourselves receive no satisfaction at all but are left emotionally empty, so to speak. The sacrifice which we have offered to God is gone.

God has no pleasure in any work which is void of sacrifice, that is to say, if it is a work which is not wholly sacrificed to Him. The issue lies not in what I have done but whether or not the work which I have done has been given up to God as a total sacrifice—whether or not what I have done shall have been completely transmitted from my hand to His. If what you and I have done fails to be totally transferred to the other party—that is, to the Lord—then it cannot be considered to have been a priestly service; therefore, that work lies outside the realm of priestly ministry in the house of God.

The two ministries, of prophet and priest were separated during Old Testament times, they having been placed in different persons. For example, Moses, Samuel, Isaiah, and others were prophets, whereas Aaron and his sons were priests serving in the house of God. In coming to the New Testament era, however, we see that some believers had placed in them *both* prophetic and priestly ministries; such, for instance, like those few prophets-teachers belonging to the church in Antioch—each of whom served the Lord in both capacities in fulfilling their priestly calling.

Ministry Is Directly Related to the Lord, Not to the Church

We should understand that all our works and services today must be primarily for the Lord and thus are directly related to Him; no work is directly related to the church. Though we work and serve in the church, our works of service do not have any direct relationship to the church but are directly related to the *Head* of the church. It is the Lord who assigns the work to us, so it is He whom we serve.

114

This can be illustrated by using the example of a person's two hands. My left hand frequently helps my right hand and vice versa, do they not? For instance, the right hand cannot carry a big chair alone, so the left hand will quite naturally come to the aid of the left hand, and thus a task is accomplished. With respect to my left hand, it is not serving my right hand but is serving my head; and hence, it can be said that the work of my left hand is directly related to my head. Can we now see this?

Therefore, all the works of service which can truly support the church must be related directly to serving the Lord, for priests—if believers are truly priests—are those who serve the Lord directly because their ministry is offered up to the Lord himself who is the Head of the church. Accordingly, in the church, whether you are preaching the gospel, teaching God's word, edifying the believers, feeding the lambs, visiting the sick, even performing such works as cleaning the meeting place or serving the table: all such works of service must be done in relationship to the Lord the Head because you and I are serving Him directly and not the church.

Ministry Must Be on Resurrection Basis

Our service to God as priests must not only be directly related to Him but must also be carried out according to the principle of resurrection. This we can find confirmed in the early history of the children of Israel. God's original desire was for all the children of Israel to be priests in order that they might become a kingdom of priests (Exodus 19:6). Not long after God had delivered them out of Egypt, however, they rebelled against Him by commencing to worship the golden calf idol (Exodus 32) and later by stirring up His wrath further by even committing adultery with foreign women (Numbers 25).

Now because Phinehas, son of Eleazar and grandson of Aaron the priest, was jealous with the jealousy of God over the adulterous and idol-worshiping Israelites who had rebelled against Jehovah God, the Lord granted His covenant of forgiveness and peace to Israel; but only with Phinehas and his descendants did the Lord God make a covenant of an everlasting priesthood (Numbers 25:10-13). God, of course, had at Sinai earlier chosen Aaron and his descendants to perform the priestly ministry instead of it to have been originally the ministry of the entire congregation of Israel. One day Korah, a member of one of the clans of Levi, along with Dathan, Abiram, and other members of the tribe of Reuben, rose up against Moses and Aaron, accusing them of having lifted themselves up over the entire Israelite assembly. They wondered aloud why they should not all be priests. What then happened to them was an incident of life and death: the ground opened its mouth and swallowed all of them alive.

It should be clearly understood here that the point of controversy between Korah and his party versus Moses and Aaron was not over any other issue except that of serving God—the priesthood (Numbers 16:10). And it should be carefully noted that the moment when God punished them was at the moment of their serving God with incense at the Tent of Meeting's altar; it was not at the time of their having sinned (vv. 16-18). This truly was an awesome affair.

Korah, Dathan, and the rest of their party (over 250 people altogether) had presumed that if Aaron could minister to God as priest, why could they not do the same? But God's word shows us that the criterion for man to be priest depends neither upon his natural condition nor upon any natural requirement but solely upon his standing on the principle of resurrection. From the further narrative of this awesome event, given in Numbers 17:1-8, we glean the fact that Aaron was qualified to be priest before God because of his dead rod having budded, which unique development among all twelve tribal rods signified the presence of the principle of death and resurrection having accounted for what happened to Aaron's rod. When a branch remains on a tree, it is alive; once it is cut off, however, it becomes a dead stick or rod. Yet Aaron's rod not only budded,

116

it also produced blossoms, and even bore ripe almonds. By means of this result God was pointing out to the entire Israelite community that Aaron had been chosen by Him to be priest to serve Him. Therefore, we can rightly conclude here that to be God's priest is not that which lies within the realm of the natural but which purely lies within the realm of the supernatural—that is to say, that God's priest is one who stands on the ground of resurrection.

Hebrews chapter 7 informs us of this: "who [Christ] hath been made [priest], not after the law of a carnal commandment, but after the power of an endless life: for it is witnessed of him, Thou art a priest for ever after the order of Melchizedek" (vv. 16-17). Christ alone has been made priest with such an oath, that He is a priest forever. Christ Jesus ever lives; and consequently, His priesthood is unchangeable (vv. 20-24).

In reading the Old Testament narrative concerning Aaron's budded rod, we realize that this true physical event serves as only a symbol or type of the principle of death and resurrection. Moreover, bear in mind that the ministry of the priests among the children of Israel was always interrupted by death; therefore, their priesthood could not continue forever (see again v.23). But Christ became priest in accordance with the power of an endless life (see again v.16). The priesthood of the Old Testament era was meant, among other purposes, to serve as type, symbol or representation of the Priesthood to come, even the real and true priesthood of Christ. Today, we New Testament-era believers are made priests to serve God on the basis of Christ's resurrection life.

Inward Ministry

There is still another aspect to priestly ministry which we must consider. In serving God as priest the believer must be in touch with God and meet Him inwardly. The high priest of old needed to wear the breastplate of judgment while in the sanctuary before he could come out to manage things. Back

117

then, however busy Aaron might have been, he could not leave the tent or tabernacle of the testimony during the days of his ministry. This indicates that a priest today must shut himself in before God, for without this daily inward-dwelling experience with God there cannot be any true outward ministry. Therefore, we who are God's servants must first serve Him inwardly, drawing near to Him and communing with Him, and then emerge and go forth to work for Him.

Four—The Iniquity of the Sanctuary

And Jehovah said to Aaron, Thou and thy sons and thy fathers' house with thee shall bear the iniquity of the sanctuary; and thou and thy sons with thee shall bear the iniquity of your priesthood (Numbers 18:1).

God's word in the Old Testament informs us that some people's sins were committed in the course of their worldly lives and some were committed before God himself. Some sins were committed against common law whereas others were done against the sanctuary. We may phrase it another way, that some sins were those committed in life and some were those committed in the course of a person's work. With respect to this latter class of sins, the book of Numbers identifies for us that the sin which the priests back then had committed in the course of their work was called the iniquity of the sanctuary.

Putting this in modern terms, we may say that it is that sin which a servant of God commits in his work. People at large commit sins in their lives, but those who serve the Lord may sometimes commit outward sins. In other words, most sins committed by believers are general in nature, but God's servants may commit a special kind of sin—most notably that committed in the carrying out of their spiritual work. This is what I wish to pay special attention to here. Sins committed in the course of a servant's work are not those which we generally refer to—those such as pride, jealousy, envy, and so forth. What

118

is in view here, in contrast to that kind of sins, would be the manifestation of a little flesh, of self-will, a careless word uttered, or a thoughtless opinion expressed; such sins like these are what could be considered as special sins committed in one's work of service to the Lord. Those saints who do not serve God in a special way do not, generally speaking, commit the iniquity of the sanctuary; all those who serve, however, face the possibility of adding this special sin to their commitment of sins. The sin committed in spiritual work is that which is against God's holiness, glory, and sovereignty.

I frequently remind myself and others that there are three essential aspects to God's work which we must never forget. First, the originator of God's work must be God himself; second, the operation of God's work must be according to His power, not according to one's own power; and third, the outcome of God's work must be His glory and not man's. Any failure to observe any one of these essentials is the iniquity of the sanctuary. No work should begin with and by one's own self; no work should be done in one's own strength; and no work should end in one's own glory. Let us consider each one of these essentials in some detail.

The Origin of Divine Work Must Be God, Not Self

In a local church meeting the sisters' heads are covered in relation to the brothers. Such observance is meant to underscore the truth that every head must be covered before Christ; for He is Lord and He alone is Head, and He is therefore worthy to be Head of all. He alone is worthy to commence any work. I have not the slightest right to start anything. In short, the will of God must be the only origin of His work that is carried out by His servants.

I am tempted to ask those who are responsible in the churches: In your locality, do you start to do a work because (1) it is the opinion of the majority, (2) the thing itself is quite reasonable, and (3) the result to be had seems to be good? Or are you able to say that you are going to do a given work because you know it is the will of God? Brethren, let us realize and acknowledge that whatever is started by one's self-idea is in God's eyes an iniquity of the sanctuary. This is because in the spiritual realm we have absolutely no ground to order anything to be done out of our own thought. God has no need to have you as His brain. We read in the book of Job that God inquired of Job: "Who is this that darkeneth counsel by words without knowledge? ... and I will demand of thee, and inform thou me." (38:2, 3b).

If a work is truly spiritual, and if God is pleased to accept it, how much is its value in the end? For nothing of a work's value in the sight of God is determined by how much work you have done; it is only determined by how much of a work has or has not been started by you yourself. The less you yourself begin a work of service to God, the more spiritual, more valuable, and more acceptable it is to Him. I thank God that I have no need to start any work, since He is the one to make all decisions along that line. I am not responsible to originate anything.

Oh, how often we argue among ourselves as to how best to accomplish a work; yet God has His own thought on the matter. We need not be God's counsellors. All we need to be responsible in doing is to keep His will. It is important to make sure that the matter at hand is to be observed or undertaken according to His will. We have no need to worry about the result. The origin of God's work must be the will of God, nothing more nor less than His will.

I am fearful lest my fellow workers are not serious enough in rightly approaching the work of the sanctuary. Perhaps when you first begin to serve, you are probably quite careful, but later on you grow quite lax and careless in your approach to, and implementation of, the work of the sanctuary. Having assumed more authority with the passage of time, you tend to speak and manage more. Probably those who are just beginning to serve in the work of God are more careful than the workers who have been serving for eight or ten years.

The book of Numbers points out that there are things holy and things common. We nonetheless should not allow a thing that looks common to fall into unholiness. Have you ever baptized people? When you administer baptism the first time, you take it seriously; but after doing it five or ten times, it may become common to you.

As a further example of this danger, let us notice what the priests during Old Testament times were required to do day in and day out in the sanctuary: changing the shewbread, adding oil, burning incense, and so forth. There was nothing new to be done there on either a daily or monthly basis. Yet, a slight carelessness on the priests' part in handling those many holy things could cause them to commit the iniquity of the sanctuary and might even incur the penalty of death for themselves. Hence, none of those priests dared to treat their work of service as common.

When a worker preaches the first time, he is usually very serious; but later on, after having preached many times, he might gradually commence treating the work of preaching God's holy word as a common activity. People often say to me in this regard, "You are ever ready to preach at any time." But I want to testify that each time I am going to preach, each time it seems to me to be a difficult matter to convince myself that I have not read the New Testament sufficiently or that I have not preached on a given passage of God's word before. Brethren, concerning all of God's works which we may undertake, we should never treat them as common. If we should begin to be careless, we may most likely become sick or even experience death, for God will not allow such sin to occur without incurring chastening. On the contrary, this kind of sin will be judged at the judgment seat of Christ (II Corinthians 5:10). I am fully aware that before the judgment seat there is no sin deemed more serious than the iniquity of the sanctuary.

Brethren, we must be sober about this. We must not loosely decide on starting any work. No one should be satisfied with any work of service unless it satisfies God's will. Likewise, God himself can only be satisfied when His will is done. Apart from doing the will of God, we have no other choice. We cannot substitute for God's will anything else. All the sacrifices of the world cannot serve as an alternative to the will of God. Too often we may even think that our work surpasses God's will. We may even presume to think at times that His will is probably wrong.

Let us consider the breaking of bread—the Lord's Table— as an example. On the first occasion you reverently offer up thanks for the bread and cup because you take this sacrament very seriously: you dare not be complacent but truly conduct yourself as God's priest should. Unknowingly the power of God—the Spirit of God—rests upon you. But you may gradually become lax and your spiritual sense loses its keen edge. You fail to maintain a prayerful and worshipful spirit. Under such circumstances, and even if you realize that God has *not* anointed you with power, you nonetheless continue to do, but now in a careless fashion, what you have done before. Thus, you forfeit spiritual freshness and are deprived of the power of resurrection life. And the ultimate result is that you have fallen into the committing of the iniquity of the sanctuary, whose consequences or judgments are three in number. The first is the loss of the power of God's life which brings in a kind of staleness. The second is the setting in of a coming spiritual death. And the third is most likely the flowering of spiritual death itself.

The Operation of Work Must Be God's Power, Not Self Power

Now as the work of God which you have entered into proceeds forward, it requires the power of God to fully accomplish His will and purpose. In order to fulfill God's will, however, not only the beginning must be of God, the ongoing operation must also be of Him. We must never boast that our might has accomplished the work. And here I would ask the following: When we go before the Lord, can it be characterized as a returning home or a going before Him as guests? The answer hinges on whether we have come out from the Lord's presence in the first place. If in fact we *have* come forth from His presence, then we are returning home; otherwise, it would be our going before Him as guests. For us to return to heaven, we must have heretofore come out of heaven; and hence, it would be the case of our returning to heaven. Anyone who derives strength from Adam can only return to Adam, never to God. Accordingly, all who serve God must always acknowledge that His work can only be done in His power, otherwise nothing will be accepted by Him.

The Outcome of Work Must Glorify God, Not Self

Just as the origin of God's work is God's will and its operation is by His power, so its outcome must be His glory. To put it another way, it can be said that just as a work's method of operation must be spiritual, so its aim or objective must also be spiritual. If the process of arriving at God's purpose is not spiritual in character, we will commit the iniquity of the sanctuary, which in this case is a bringing in of the flesh into the sanctuary. Declared God, "... the stranger that cometh near shall be put to death" (Numbers 18:7b). You and I must always acknowledge that the accomplishing of God's work does not depend on our strength. The question needing to be asked of ourselves is not how much we have done but how much power has God given us? A brother once observed that "only that which comes from heaven may return to heaven."

Why is it that God does not permit people to be saved by works (Ephesians 2:8-9)? What is God's motive in His monopolizing the work of salvation? The answer is that He may get all the glory. The amount of works one does in service to God determines the measure which He receives of glory. It is as though God, in His concern that you may obtain His glory, does not allow His servants to be or become anything about which they could boast. For this reason, when God contemplates the accomplishing of His works, He chooses the weak, the useless, and the despised of the world "so that no flesh should boast before [Him]" (I Corinthians 1:29). God is concerned that you or I may obtain some glory. Though God is willing to give everything else to men, even His only begotten Son, He will not give His glory to them. We can only *enter into* the glory of the Lord.

You and I who are poor and weak and despised may rob God of His glory by boasting to ourselves or to others that we have helped some brothers and sisters somewhat or have been instrumental in having saved a few souls. Such conduct constitutes a robbing God of His glory. Let us recognize and ever be mindful of the fact that glory belongs only to God and not to ourselves as well.

Once after I had preached in a certain place, a brother came up to me, saying: "Brother Nee, you preached well tonight. Are you proud of it?" I did not respond at once, for I had never been asked that kind of question before. After carefully considering whether or not I was proud, I said to him, "I have never thought of this matter before. Perhaps I am very proud of this, yet I do not feel proud." I learned something that evening from this incident; which was, that if a person only seeks after God's will and only asks that God's glory be the outcome of one's service to Him, then that person will not be guilty of robbing God's glory at all. Should anyone think of grasping glory from God, it is for sure that that person has failed in seeing to it that God receives all glory.

There is another aspect to this matter which is worth pointing out; which is, that everything to be seen in the tabernacle and temple sanctuary of old spoke of the glory of God. For are we not told in the Old Testament Scriptures that the holy temple is full of God's glory? (see II Chronicles 5:14)

And in New Testament terms, it can be said that in God's holy church, everything speaks only of the glory of Christ and not of one's sacrificial service to God.

The question for today is therefore this: Who is worthy to show forth God's glory? Yes, God might have called some brothers to serve Him; yes, He could also have poured out His Spirit upon them and given them overcoming life. Indeed, I have heard of some brethren among us who have served quite well. And so, I am fearful lest any of God's servants becomes proud. Whoever fails to know God's will and fails to recognize His glory tends to depend upon his own self in his works of service to God and therefore seeks his own personal glory. I would consequently urge us all to take serious note of what God in His word has declared in response to such conduct: that the Lord God "rejects" and "resists" the proud (I Samuel 15:23, Proverbs 3:34, James 4:6, I Peter 5:5 ASV). Hence God's servants need to be reminded and warned of how easy it is for them to end up committing the sin of robbing the Lord of His glory.

No one among us wants to be considered a thief, yet stealing the Lord's glory is an act of theft. God not only demands of us to get rid of outward evil action, He also requires of us to not steal His glory. God is all good and we are all bad. We acknowledge that all goodness can only be found in the Lord, not in us (Psalm 14:1-3; 53:1-3; Mark 10:18; Luke 18:19; Romans 3:10, 12; 7:18). Stealing God's glory is the iniquity of the sanctuary. All in the sanctuary—the shewbread, the lampstand, the altar of incense, and so forth—all speak of Christ. In God's sanctuary of today, the church, there is nothing but Christ. God is unwilling for us to obtain any glory in the sanctuary. As we enter the Holiest of All, we see only the ark, which is Christ, and the cherubim above the ark who cry out: "Holy, holy, holy, the Lord God almighty" (Revelation 4:8, Exodus 25:22). If God should bring forth and reveal what is within us, we would discover how unclean we are. Whenever I have had to reprimand a brother, I go before God in fearful fashion; for my thought each time has been that if it were not due to the grace of the Lord I would be worse than that brother.

Paul confessed that but for the grace of God, he would remain what he was before he met the Lord on the road to Damascus; that even his apostleship was due to God's grace (I Corinthians 15:9-10). We naively suppose that to be an apostle is a glorious thing, not realizing that all glory belongs to God himself and that what we received is grace alone. Let us humbly acknowledge that we are not worthy of any glory. The one at the bottom cannot give grace to the one above him, for grace flows from high above to the one down below. In like manner, only the one sitting in a chair can give grace to him who is seated on the floor. For us today we can find no two words more serious than those two referenced earlier: "resist" and "reject." To be rejected is equal in meaning and effect to being finished, and "resist" is the word used against Satan (James 4:7) just after it is used against the proud (James 4:6). In God's eyes, nothing is more hateful than pride.

Throughout the entire world those people who are deceived by Satan are the proud in heart, for the proud do not know themselves. In contrast to them, all who truly know themselves will not be deceived, for as the latter come before God, they will see themselves as altogether unclean and possessing nothing of which to boast or be proud (cf. Isaiah 6:1-7). I believe that unless the blood of the Lord covers me, I dare not do any work for Him. Without the covering of His blood I cannot even be a Christian. Indeed, I ask you, Is there anything worthy in us that has not come to us by means of the grace of the Lord? Can we therefore ever think of ourselves as being better than others? We can only obtain grace, not glory.

All who have received grace today may not enter into the glory of God right now. On earth today we are the weak and the lowly, for we are like Lazarus, desirous of being filled with crumbs which fall from a rich man's table (cf. Luke 16:19-21).

We can only be receivers who truly and humbly receive grace from God.

Here, then, is something quite challenging for all the Lord's servants to avoid: that those who participate in the work of God always have the possibility of falling prey to committing the iniquity of the sanctuary. How terrible is this sin, for in reading again Numbers chapter 18 we come to realize that most sins committed in the sanctuary are those whose ultimate penalty is death; even approaching the holy place in an improper manner can be a sin which leads to death (vv. 1-7).

Back then, determining the iniquity of the sanctuary did not require the exercise of *human* judgment, because God himself was the one who judged the matter directly. For instance, any stranger who came near the sanctuary would immediately be put to death without the person being judged at all by the priest (vv. 4b, 7c). Back then, ordinary sins needed to be judged by the priest; but the iniquity of the sanctuary was viewed as a sin committed *directly* against God; and hence, God judged directly.

Many of our sins today are the case of our indirectly sinning against God, but our committing the iniquity of the sanctuary is a sin against God directly. This is because the sanctuary—the church—belongs to God, and the committing of any iniquity of the sanctuary touches His glory, that is, it touches God himself.

I can only speak or preach under the covering of the blood. If ever I fail to do so, I must ask for God's forgiveness and also for forgiveness from the brethren.

TITLES AVAILABLE
from Christian Fellowship Publishers

By Watchman Nee

Aids to "Revelation"	The Life That Wins
Amazing Grace	The Lord My Portion
Back to the Cross	The Messenger of the Cross
A Balanced Christian Life	The Ministry of God's Word
The Better Covenant	My Spiritual Journey
The Body of Christ: A Reality	The Mystery of Creation
The Character of God's Workman	Powerful According to God
Christ the Sum of All Spiritual Things	Practical Issues of This Life
The Church and the Work – 3 Vols	The Prayer Ministry of the Church
The Church in the Eternal Purpose of God	The Release of the Spirit
"Come, Lord Jesus"	Revive Thy Work
The Communion of the Holy Spirit	The Salvation of the Soul
The Finest of the Wheat – Vol. 1	The Secret of Christian Living
The Finest of the Wheat – Vol. 2	Serve in Spirit
From Faith to Faith	The Spirit of Judgment
From Glory to Glory	The Spirit of the Gospel
Full of Grace and Truth – Vol. 1	The Spirit of Wisdom and Revelation
Full of Grace and Truth – Vol. 2	Spiritual Authority
Gleanings in the Fields of Boaz	Spiritual Discernment
The Glory of His Life	Spiritual Exercise
God's Plan and the Overcomers	Spiritual Knowledge
God's Work	The Spiritual Man
Gospel Dialogue	Spiritual Reality or Obsession
Grace Abounding	Take Heed
Grace for Grace	The Testimony of God
Heart-to-Heart Talks	The Universal Priesthood of Believers
Interpreting Matthew	Whom Shall I Send?
Journeying towards the Spiritual	The Word of the Cross
The King and the Kingdom of Heaven	Worship God
The Latent Power of the Soul	Ye Search the Scriptures
Let Us Pray	

The Basic Lesson Series
Vol. 1 - A Living Sacrifice
Vol. 2 - The Good Confession
Vol. 3 - Assembling Together
Vol. 4 - Not I, But Christ
Vol. 5 - Do All to the Glory of God
Vol. 6 - Love One Another

ORDER FROM: 11515 Allecingie Parkway Richmond, VA 23235
www.c-f-p.com – 804-794-5333

TITLES AVAILABLE
from Christian Fellowship Publishers

By Stephen Kaung

"But We See Jesus"—*the Life of the Lord Jesus*
Discipled to Christ—*As Seen in the Life of Simon Peter*
God's Purpose for the Family
The Gymnasium of Christ
In the Footsteps of Christ
The Key to "Revelation" – Vol. 1
The Key to "Revelation" – Vol. 2
New Covenant Living & Ministry
Now We See the Church—*the Life of the Church, the Body of Christ*
Shepherding
The Songs of Degrees—*Meditations on Fifteen Psalms*
The Splendor of His Ways—*Seeing the Lord's End in Job*

The "God Has Spoken" Series
Seeing Christ in the Old Testament, Part One
Seeing Christ in the Old Testament, Part Two
Seeing Christ in the New Testament

ORDER FROM: 11515 Allecingie Parkway Richmond, VA 23235
www.c-f-p.com – 804-794-5333